D0106684

PAINFUL PEOPLE

AND HOW TO DEAL WITH THEM

Joseph Dunn

HarperCollins*Publishers*

HarperCollins*Publishers*

First published in Australia in 1997
Reprinted in 1997
by HarperCollins*Publishers* Pty Limited
ACN 009 913 517
A member of the HarperCollins*Publishers* (Australia) Pty Limited Group
http://www.harpercollins.com.au

Copyright © Dr Joseph Dunn, 1997

This book is copyright.
Apart from any fair dealing for the purposes of private study, research,
criticism or review, as permitted under the Copyright Act, no part may
be reproduced by any process without written permission.
Inquiries should be addressed to the publishers.

HarperCollins*Publishers*
25 Ryde Road, Pymble, Sydney, NSW 2073, Australia
31 View Road, Glenfield, Auckland 10, New Zealand
77-85 Fulham Palace Road, London W6 8JB, United Kingdom
Hazelton Lanes, 55 Avenue Road, Suite 2900, Toronto, Ontario M5R 3L2
and 1995 Markham Road, Scarborough, Ontario M1B 5M8, Canada
10 East 53rd Street, New York NY 10032, USA

National Library of Australia Cataloguing-in-Publication data:

Dunn, Joe, 1955– .
Painful people; and how to deal with them.
ISBN 0 7322 5737 9.
I. Title.
616.858

Cover illustration by Liam Hillier
Internal illustration by Liam Hillier
Printed in Australia by Griffin Press on 79gsm Bulky Paperback

9 8 7 6 5 4 3 2   97 98 99

To Susan and our children
Joni, Tom, Liam, Harry
and Gaby.

CONTENTS

CHAPTER I

AN INTRODUCTION TO PAINFUL PEOPLE . . .

You probably know plenty of Painful People already! So why should you bother to read about them? This book will help you to understand just why the Painful People you already know are so damned *painful*.

My own introduction to the fascinating field of personality pathology (or what makes people painful) occurred when I was a medical student. That was too many years ago for me to remember without shuddering. My psychiatry lectures were given by a tall thin boffin of a psychiatrist who had no sense of humour and wore dark suits. He might just as well have been an undertaker.

At the start of the lecture entitled 'Personality Disorders' he warned us that we should resist the temptation to start diagnosing all sorts of mental pathology in our family and our classmates. He was right of course. For the next hour we all looked around the lecture theatre at each other with realisation on our faces, nodding wisely.

Many years later I lost my sense of humour, wore dark suits and became a psychiatrist myself. People often ask me how the funeral business is going. Now when I see a new patient my first thought is 'What is this patient's *personality*?' This is the first key to understanding why they are painful – or pain-full.

It comes before any consideration of their emotional state, their biology or why they hate their mothers. You see, our personalities can get us into a lot of trouble. They can strain all our relationships, make us live in a state of barely controlled torment or stop us from 'getting on' in life – you know, maturity, marriage, mortgage, maternity clothes, mortuaries, etc. Our personalities can also get us out of trouble if we are reasonably highly functioning individuals.

When I recently gave a seminar to a group about how to stay sane in the crazy world of business I found that talking about the categorisation of personalities was the subject that really woke them up. Up until then they must have thought that I was teaching them about burial rites or something. But all of a sudden they began to scan the seminar room with looks of realisation on their faces, and to nod wisely . . . So learning about personality is not just for psychiatrists.

There are three parts to this book. I call them the 'three Ps':

♦ The first part is about paradigms. The crux here is that people are so complicated that there is no single way of viewing them. In the paradigms I show that there are (at least) ten things to consider when trying to find a pigeonhole for a particular personality. Confused? Don't worry. When you read this part it'll click.

♦ The second part is about *personalities*. There are some people who go through life inflicting pain on everyone around them. And there are some people who go through life quietly, never saying a word of complaint about their torment. You'll find both types under this section. It's about how people's personalities, usually through no fault of their own, go a bit wonky. If you find yourself described here, don't be too hard on yourself: none of us has a squeaky-clean personality.

♦ The third part is about predicaments. We all encounter a few 'predicaments' in our lives. They are the painful things that are thrust upon us: losses, abuse, mental illness. But beneath them all is the underlying theme of personality: stronger people, and people who derive good support from their relationships, often do better at managing these predicaments.

Before we get on with the nitty-gritty, bear with me as I emphasise two points. These are necessary so that the mere act of reading this book does not inflict pain upon the reader. By the time you finish this book you are supposed to *know* about Painful People, not *be* one. So pay attention:

♦ The first point is that the 'case histories' in the book describe characters who are figments of my fertile imagination. They are described, quite simply, to emphasise a point. On the other hand, if you recognise nothing of yourself in any of the case histories then you are fooling yourself. Or a bloody saint.

♦ The second point is that I am not very 'politically correct'. I refuse to refer to Guy Chapman as Person Personperson. When the people described in *personalities* and *predicaments* are referred to as 'him' or 'her' that is, quite simply, because most of the people who suffer from that particular 'p' are either 'hims' or 'hers'. This is not because I am planning to water-bomb the next women's rights march or charge through a men's group meeting shouting comments that question their virility. It's just simpler that way.

Enough of the preamble. Let's get on with the 'Ps'.

CHAPTER 2

SO WHAT'S A PARADIGM?

It took me years to understand what a paradigm was so if you can get it in a sentence you're doing well. So here goes. A paradigm is a way of viewing something. There, simple wasn't it.

Okay, okay. Maybe that definition was a little too, well, simple. A paradigm is a perspective, the basis of a school of thought, a dialect. A way of viewing something. To cut to the quick — and so you can get that confused look off your face — let me give you an example. Let's talk about *time*.

consider this

You're a high-flying businessman. When you're driving to work or hanging around the first-class lounges at airports you're only too aware of the time. It's a linear thing. From the future it comes into that infinitely small moment called the present and then disappears into the past. You can mark places along this continuum to create time for meetings, re-create significant moments from the past in anniversaries and do some projective planning about some other places in time in the future. You even have a digital watch. No longer is time something that sweeps slowly but inexorably past twelve numbers. It is now a display of ever-changing numbers.

Ah, numbers. You're comforted by them. They are so crisp. Pristine. Some nerd in a white coat somewhere in a laboratory with white walls and fluorescent lighting once worked out that a second was so many hundreds of thousands of oscillations of some microscopic particle – just in case you ever wondered. So time is concrete and reliable. And your digital watch reminds you that it can be measured so precisely as it marches down the sweetly simple unidimensional line from the future to the present and into the past. And that's the way your life will be lived. From the beginning to the end, which is called 'death'. Why can't everything be so simple?

now consider this

You are a woman and you live in the East. Not the eastern suburbs, dingbat, but a country in Asia. You know all about time. It is a circular, recurring thing like the ripples from a stone tossed into a pond. When the seasons come and go you know how recurring time is. And so is your menstrual cycle. And your life. You believe that after the end of this life you'll be reborn into an almost never-ending cycle of birth and death. In the West we only obliquely acknowledge this circularity. The French say *'plus ca change, plus c'est la meme chose'* (the more things change, the more they remain the same). In English we say that the person who does not understand history is condemned to repeat it.

and now consider this

You are an astrophysicist. When people ask you 'Where does the universe end?' and 'Where are the boundaries of space?' you smile your knowing smile and are thankful that you understand what dimensions and fractals are. You live in the world of reductionism. You want to reduce things, especially life, the world and all that stuff, into the simplest possible terms. If things are complex that's just because you don't understand the simplicity beneath it all. When astrophysical push comes to cosmological shove, there are only two dimensions that you worry about. They are matter/energy and space/time. Matter/energy is quite straightforward. Matter can be converted into energy. Nuclear weapons demonstrate that in an unambiguous way.

So what is this thing called time? Well, when three-dimensional space curls over at its boundaries, it becomes time. See? Just as simple as a definition of 'paradigm'. Yes, when you're late for work you think that time is linear. And when you see the beauty of the falling brown leaves from the oak trees outside your observatory window you know that the seasons come in a cyclical fashion. But you also know that time is simply a useful concept for the feeble human mind so that we know that the day can be measured and three hundred and sixty-five and a quarter days have some sort of celestial significance.

So that's what a paradigm is. It's a way of viewing something. Time can be viewed as a linear construct that can be accurately measured by digital watches. Or it can be viewed as a cyclical, recurring phenomenon. Or it can be viewed as one of the four building blocks of the everything that we call the universe: matter, energy, space and our old friend time.

It just depends upon what *paradigm* you use.

people paradigms

You are about to launch into the part of the book that describes the paradigms that are used to describe people. Each of these is a slightly different dialect in people-speak. So why are they necessary? They're necessary because people are just *so damned complicated*. If people were simple like, say, garden slugs, then people in my profession wouldn't spend hours writing books like this. Okay?

Stick with me. You'll understand in just a few pages.

The pain paradigm: painful versus pain-full

> The question to be asked: Does this person punish inwardly or outwardly?

Not all the people described in this book are truly 'painful'. In one of those strange little quirks of the English language the word that implies that people carry pain usually indicates that these same people do a pretty good job of inflicting the aforementioned pain onto everyone around them. Other people who are in pain keep it to themselves. Those people are 'pain-full'.

The former group (painful) are called 'extrapunitive'; the latter group (pain-full) are called 'intrapunitive'. The former group punish others; the latter group punish themselves. The former group are noisy and provocative; the latter group suffer in silence. Both are included in this book but you need to get the difference right.

consider this

You're a teenager who is heavily into rap music. You can't for the life of you imagine why all the world doesn't share your passion. You decide that it is your job to educate the world in the pleasures of rap music. You will play it loudly on your ghetto blaster when you're in your bedroom (your mother's passionate about Mozart and your father's passionate about opera) and you will play it loudly at the beach. You will play it walking down the street. Some of your friends are getting sick of it but you'll convert them anyway. You have taken rap music and turned it into a weapon. You're now *painful*. But don't worry. Somewhere in your mid-twenties it will dawn on you what a jerk you've been . . .

now consider this

You're a delinquent. You didn't ask to be one but a combination of dyslexia, having a mother who continually reminded you that your conception was 'a mistake' and getting in with a really welcoming bunch of people who steal cars has made you what you are. You don't have a television because you can't afford one. So you break into someone's home and pinch theirs. When they come home they have a horrible feeling that they have just been raped.

One day, in the middle of a house break-in you realise that the woman of the house is still home. She comes into the room. For a moment you look at each other. You think that you could rape her. But then you would have to kill her so that she couldn't identify you in one of those line-ups down at the police station. You change your mind and run out of the house as fast as you can. In a few years' time you will be bitter and twisted enough to carry the rape thing through.

Sure you carry a lot of pain. But you will spend your life inflicting it on others.

You're heartily sick of coming home to find that your television set has been pinched. You want to give those lazy incompetent cops a wake-up call. After all, what do you pay all these taxes for? You join a demonstration march to denounce crime and encourage the police to get off their backsides and patrol your neighbourhood. You want to 'reclaim the night'. You stop traffic. You shout and chant with loudhailers. Someone throws an egg at those bums in blue uniforms. You jeer as the egg-thrower is handcuffed and led away.

See? Just about anyone can be *painful*. All they have to do is carry enough pain and it spills over. When you well and truly hate some painful idiot, when you could gladly fling him from a cliff, keep in mind that he has his pain too.

You are a woman of svelte proportions. Except your feet. They're great big plates of meat.

The problem is that your husband is taking you to a ball tonight and you're supposed to look like Cinderella. How can any self-respecting *belle* whirl around the dance floor when she looks as if she should be bushwalking? You plan to sit at your table most of the night so that you can hide your feet under the tablecloth. And you force them into a pair of high heels that are about one-and-a-half sizes too small.

At the end of the evening you prise off your dainty dancing shoes and then spend the next few days learning how to walk again. The tragedy is that no one in the ballroom even noticed your feet. It's all in your head. You have put on a brave face while masking your intense podiatric self-consciousness. You're truly *pain-full*.

And now consider this

You're a businessman. You're in the middle of making a crucial presentation to the board of directors. You've been preparing for this for months. Now is your big chance. Either you'll convince them to spend a fortune on your project or you'll fade away into corporate obscurity.

The problem is that you shouldn't have had that chilli octopus at the restaurant for dinner last night. It's playing havoc with your bowels. You've already rushed to the loo three times this morning. You're rapidly discovering what a vengeful little creature the octopus is.

But you soldier on bravely during your presentation because you will look like a one hundred per cent pure buffoon if you do a runner for the toilet just as you get to the bit about projected expenditure. No one notices how pale you look or how you're blurting out your words staccato-style. You have joined the ranks of the *pain-full*.

Here ends the first paradigm. It's all about pain. And who inflicts it on whom. When you're thinking about personalities try to work out where the pain is going. Some people are *painful*; others are *pain-full*; most are both.

The pathology paradigm: pathology versus physiology

> The question to be asked: Are this person's personality traits pathological?

Medical school is six years of intellectual torture. So why am I telling you that? Because I'm feeling pain-full and trying to elicit sympathy. And also because I'm trying to make a point.

Take a look at any medical school anywhere in the world and you will find a pattern in the teaching program. The first two or three years are for teaching physiology. The second two or three years are for teaching pathology. Physiology is about how the organ systems in the body are supposed to work. Pathology is about how it all goes wrong. Physiology is about normality and pathology is about disease.

Now try to apply this to personalities. This is what psychiatrists do when we talk about 'personality disorder'. Barristers often try to pin us down when we're in the witness box. 'Doctor, do you believe that my client suffers from a *personality disorder*?' When you're in the box this question makes your heart sink. And the barrister knows you're wriggling.

You see, defining what constitutes a personality disorder is clinically very useful but unfortunately quite impossible. No one has an entirely 'normal' personality. We all have our warts and foibles. So just how many warts and how many foibles do you need to make the grade? When it comes to personality when does physiology stop and pathology start?

To the rescue come two concepts. They are called the two 'Ds'. That stands for *distress* and *dysfunction*. People who have personality disorders usually show their unfortunate, sometimes obnoxious, personality traits from late adolescence. While they can mellow as they get older they usually never quite stop being either painful or pain-full. But the true test of a person whose personality is *disordered* are the Ds:

- ◆ *distress* implies that the person carries more than their fair share of pain
- ◆ *dysfunction* implies that they are unable to get on in life, to mature and to accomplish the usual goals of life.

So far so good. But then let's get real here. The line between physiology and pathology remains blurred. Some degree of personality pathology is inevitable and 'incurable'. Only do-gooders and religious zealots like to think that they're perfect. Life is an inherently painful process and no one asked us whether we wanted to be conceived. But as they say in the gangster movies, 'them's the breaks'.

Now hang on to these two points:

- ◆ when it comes to pathological personality traits, it's all a matter of degree
- ◆ it is more efficient to remedy personality pathology than to try to create super-physiology.

Confused? Good. Now read on.

You're obsessive about tidiness. You like to have everything in its place and you're always precisely punctual. Your presentation is always immaculate. Not a hair out of place. You look as if you wake from sleep without a single crushed curl. For you life would be hell-on-earth if you had to live in a messy house or were late to appointments.

Time and space. If you have to live in them then you might as well master them. But what you won't own up to is that time and space have mastered you. You have lost the ability to be flexible. You have lost the fine art of laziness. Your world is neat, tidy and sterile.

now consider this

The person who invented the term 'slob' had you in mind. Your bedroom bears a striking resemblance to the local rubbish tip. You're thirty-eight years old but somehow you got stuck in a slothful adolescent phase. You dread your annual bath. You can't keep a job because hypertensive supervisors go red with rage when you habitually show up late. People think you're on drugs all the time because you're so bereft of enthusiasm. But this is just you. And the only things going for you are that your stomach is ulcer-free and you won't die of a heart attack.

So get the point. People who are too obsessional go through life feeling relentlessly uptight. People who are not obsessional enough have difficulty getting anywhere. Or at least getting there on time.

It's all a matter of degree.

Take notice that the same principle applies to being selfish, being suspicious, being dependent, etc. Not too much, not too little.

now consider this

You are a businessman. You are depressed as all hell, but no one knows. Not even you. You think that you are just a little 'burned-out'. At Friday night drinks your colleagues detect that you're not your cheerful self so they ply you with alcohol. It gives a few moments of relief from your abject misery and then a powerful hangover. You battle it through even though the boss takes you aside for one of his irritating little 'pep talks'.

You've been using your affirmations to try to motivate yourself but you've felt as if you've been putting your foot on the accelerator but leaving the hand-brake on. What a pity. If you had had the guts to sit down with someone who could put an appropriate label onto your misery then something could be done about it. But you could never ever admit that there was something wrong with your mind. What would people think?

and now consider this

Your company sends you to a seminar on motivation. You sit in a huge auditorium. On the back of an envelope you calculate that the organisers of the seminar must be making about $30 000 out of this and they do it three times a week. Nice work if you can get it.

An athletic-looking man with an American accent parades up and down on the stage talking at you. His energy is contagious. Then the audience participation starts. Cheers, thrills, tears. Pretty punchy stuff. You leave the auditorium that evening on cloud nine. You have motivation oozing from every pore. You are going to slay the world. You deserve it. You were born to greatness. Your salary is a pittance compared to what you deserve and you're going to thump your boss's desk in the morning.

Six days later you're all stale again. Your boss told you to go thump a tree. You know now that you were born to be in middle management. The bubble has burst.

So get the message. In the business world people are continually trying to create 'superstaff': employees who will run on double the average work output, 365 days a year.

Now your boss needs to get real. It would be far more efficient for him to go through his staff and weed out the personal pathology that is always there. It's just that he turns a blind eye to it. Weeding works much better than trying to whip along 'superstaff' who can never sustain their enthusiasm. Efficiency is about reducing pathology, not creating super-physiology.

One final thought. In all this talk about personality pathology you might get the impression that humanity is a pack of thieves, pests and fools. Far from it. Let me quote to you Dunn's Law. It states that:

'*Most* people are *mostly* good *most* of the time.'

Yes, it follows that some people are mostly bad all of the time and all people are partly bad most of the time. But Dunn's Law still stands. Don't forget it.

PARADIGM 3

The medical paradigm: psychiatry versus neurology

> The question to be asked: Is the problem in this person's mind or in their brain?

Remember Plato? You know, dialectic and sandals. He gave us the term 'platonic relationship'. Poor Plato. He must have had a lousy sex life.

Plato did his writing long before anatomy laboratories and electron microscopes were invented. Yet he summed up in three words what the mind does: it thinks, it feels and it wants. Simple as that. Except he called the processes reason (for cognition, or thinking), passion (for emotion) and appetite (for wanting, or 'conation').

Years after Plato died, someone dreamed up the idea that medicine was becoming so complex and so beyond the realm of mere mortals to understand that some doctors should become *specialised* in one particular field. Hence the world became populated with tribes called, for example, 'paediatricians' and 'dermatologists'. One of the tribes was called 'neurologists' and they were the brainiest of all, in more ways than one.

Neurologists are medical specialists who know how your brain and nervous system work. When you have a stroke or a brain injury or one of those rare, progressive fatal disorders that beautiful women in romantic movies die of, then you're probably going to end up seeing a neurologist.

Around a hundred years ago doctors made a brave step. Up until then it had never occurred to anyone that neurosis and madness were anything to do with medicine. They were simply part of the human condition and they were spoken of to clergymen or confidantes. Doctors, on the other hand, laid no claim to any mental process, just body stuff. Until, that is, doctors like Josef Breuer and Sigmund Freud came along. Bingo! Psychiatry was discovered and there was no going back. Now medicine had to consider the mind, its thoughts, feelings and desires. In other words, Plato was back in fashion. And ever since that day we psychiatrists have been scrambling to be recognised as part of the white-coat-and-stethoscope brigade.

So what has all this got to do with Painful People? Plenty. Read on.

We live in a world where neurologists lay claim to the brain and psychiatrists lay claim to the mind. Did you spot the obvious mistake. Right! There's a problem with that demarcation. The mind and all its mental experiences come from the brain. Brain death equals no thoughts or feelings or desires. Brain injury means that all those processes go a bit wonky. So how do neurologists and psychiatrists know when they are standing on each other's professional toes?

E X E R C I S E

❶ Take a human brain. Preferably not your own. There's some dissection involved here.

❷ Now cut off the frontal lobes. In order to find them draw a line across the top of the head from ear to ear. The frontal lobes are those big bulbous things forward of your ear-to-ear line. Now chop them off. Whoever you're doing this to has just lost all their ability to work out what they want and to go for it. Frontal lobes are important for 'executive skills'. That doesn't refer to the numbers that the psychologist puts onto your personality test. It refers to the way in which we human beings work out what we want to do or be or have and get on with accomplishing these goals.

When frontal lobotomy was all the rage the process of cutting off frontal lobes was supposed to leave people free from the torment of their mental illness. Sometimes people who had had 'the chop' lived the rest of their days in a state of benign apathy. At least they didn't worry about getting a surprise visit from the taxation department any more.

Frontal lobes give us our get up and go. They make us be able to plan things. They give us lots of those traits that have come to be called 'personality'. Useful things, frontal lobes. Hang onto them.

❸ Now back to the dissection.

Go to that part of the brain that is directly behind the nose. It sits on the underside of the brain. This is the most primitive part of the brain. Now scrape it all out.

If your subject is still breathing, that's a bonus. You see, this primitive part of the brain also serves such handy things as heart function, breathing, sleep, hunger, thirst, etc. It is also where your emotions come from. It is called the 'diencephalon'. Your subject, now diencephalon-free, will be liberated forever from the burden of emotion. Perhaps this is what happened to Mr Spock . . .

❹ Now we have to stop the subject from thinking. This function is carried out in the cerebral cortex. That's the 'skin' of the brain. Thinking goes on in the last few layers of cells on the very outside of the brain. Now peel the brain as if you were peeling an orange that's made of avocado. There! No more thoughts. Ever. Of course the other way that you can do this is to give someone a dose of Alzheimer's disease. Except that takes years.

❺ Now give whatever is left of the brain to a neurologist. This is their share. They can do with it as they please. We psychiatrists can have the bits in the bucket.

Just before you turn a pale shade of green, let me remind you that there is method in my – er – madness. I am trying to confront you with something that you have always wondered about: why do psychiatrists have to become medical practitioners before they specialise in psychiatry?

The answer is that psychiatrists must have sound working knowledge of the whole brain because sometimes disorders present to psychiatrists that are more to do with the brain than the mind. They are called the *organic* disorders. Organic disorders of the mind are those in which there is a readily identifiable disease or 'insult' to the brain that is causing the abnormality of mind.

Keep in mind that the brain is an electrochemical computer that floats in a soup of hormones and is encased in a box of bone. It comes as no surprise that things go wrong with it and even less surprise that it's hard to get at to study. Here are some *organic* disorders:

CASE HISTORY

Alan was a nice bloke when he was sober but a prize pain in the backside when he was drunk. As every successive beer passed his lips he would take one step away from the Dr Hyde and one step closer to the Mr Jekyll. While sloshed he would go through an entire personality change. No more meek and mild. He became sarcastic, demanding, domineering and eventually violent.

After years of Jekylling like this he began to undergo a permanent organic personality change. He began to dement. That means that the alcohol had been punishing his brain cells too much for too long. His frontal lobes and his cerebral cortex began to do a disappearing act. He ended up as a shrivelled little old man with a really nasty streak, living in a nursing home and waiting to die. Sober at last, but too late.

CASE HISTORY

This is a real one. In 1966 a character named Charles Whitman decided that he was going to go on a killing rampage. He climbed the clock tower at the University of Texas and used a sniper's rifle with telescopic sight to shoot forty-seven people who wandered into his range. Sixteen of them died.

What followed would have made Arnold Schwarzenegger proud. A whole lot of gun-toting American policemen descended upon Whitman and ended his murder spree by shooting him to bits. Literally. When the forensic pathologists studied what was left of his brain they made an interesting discovery: he had an amygdaloid tumour. That's the part of your brain that regulates aggressive behaviour. Whitman looked really angry and really mad but maybe he just had a rare and weird brain cancer.

CASE HISTORY

Brian was driving to work when a big green truck in his way brought him to a sudden and complete halt. Brian should have had an airbag but he was middle-aged and so was his car. It had been built in pre-airbag days. His frontal lobes met the steering wheel with some considerable force and the only thing that stopped them from decorating the windscreen was his wrinkled forehead.

Two months in intensive care for him and four months of painstaking rehabilitation later, Brian's wife was becoming increasingly worried. Brian had emerged from his coma a changed man. But a nasty change. Brian oscillated between apathy and provocative disinhibition. Frontal lobe damage. Subtle but devastating.

The take-home message here is that not all aspects of personality are related to neglect or abuse. Sometimes personalities change because you have just poisoned your brain. Or clobbered it. This is where neurologists and psychiatrists co-operate in treating the same patient.

The Taoist paradigm: care versus control

> The question to be asked: How does this person balance care and control in their lives?

Taoism is a religious/philosophical movement that sprang up in China as long ago as 4500 BC. We're not talking about some fad here.

Taoism has as its core a belief in dual forces in the universe. They are called 'yin' and 'yang'. Yin is the female force that pervades everything that is light, soft, yielding and caring. Yang is the male force that pervades everything that is dark, hard, penetrating and controlling.

The circular symbol that epitomises this duality appears on the Korean flag. In the Western world you will occasionally see this symbol on some kid's martial arts uniform or on the wall charts at your acupuncturist. But it has plenty of relevance for understanding people, especially painful ones. The duality here is how much people care for others and how much they control others. Care and control. Control and care. They are like phallic symbols: once you know what they are you'll find them everywhere.

When observing people, note that when two people relate to each other with any degree of passion or hormone action they are usually either caring for each other or controlling each other. For 'care' read all shades of love, compassion, nurturing, feeding, nursing and parenting. For 'control' read everything to do with domination, force, manipulation or coercion.

Now let's see how this duality affects our people-watching . . .

CASE HISTORY

Christine was a nurse. She loved her work. Yes, it involved all sorts of self-sacrifice, but look at the rewards! If Christine had been born a hundred years ago then she would have been a nun or a missionary or a philanthropist. She would do anything to care for others. And get all sorts of satisfaction in return.

The problem was that she was great at looking after everyone else but not much good at looking after herself. She had learned to be selfless but needed to brush up on the universal need to be out-and-out selfish from time to time. Selfless people martyr themselves to others. Or find that other people doormat them. The moral of the story: too much care; too much self-control; not enough rebellion. Great for saints. Awful for people.

CASE HISTORY

Dennis was a bully. A dictator. A control-freak. Dennis got what Dennis wanted. Dennis could never delegate anything to anyone because no one could do anything as well as Dennis could. Dennis was a one-man standover operation. He controlled time, place, people, thought.

If Dennis sounds like your boss then you will already know how oppressive it is to live in an environment that's too controlled.

Now try to analyse what is the central theme from these snippets:

♦ Four-year-old Edward had that four-year-old tone of voice. Cute but a bit whiney. He would say 'Muuuum, can I go and . . . ?' There would always be a request for 'permission' to carry out some action. Such as eating a worm or playing in some knee-deep puddles.

♦ 'Look, Frank, let me lay my cards on the table,' said Dr Green. 'You're manic again. You should've taken your lithium but you keep turfing it down the toilet. And then you get like this: speedy, disinhibited, unable to sleep, out of control, spending too much and offending everyone. You have to go to hospital. No ifs or buts. And if you don't agree to this then I'll have no option but to call the police and commit you under the Mental Health Act. Got it?'

♦ You are driving into town in rush hour. Your journey is punctuated by mind-numbing stops that are called 'red traffic lights'. It takes you twice as long as it would if all of those bloody traffic lights weren't there. But you're a law-abiding citizen so you wait patiently at every red light, flicking through radio stations trying to find something to un-numb your mind.

Enough snippets. The moral here is that there is control inflicted upon us all the time. Often, like wee Edward, we go and look for it. Watch how human beings form groups too: they will always officially or unofficially find someone to lead them. We can't stand milling around like too many Indians and not enough chiefs.

We acknowledge that traffic lights are necessary even if they are a scourge on civilisation. They *protect* us, just like Edward's mum protects Edward. And Dr Green's attempt to heavy Frank into going into hospital is for Frank's benefit, not Dr Green's. When controlling you is for your benefit then that's called *protection*. The formula is simple:

Care + Control = Protection

Now when you are people-watching look out for the signs of care and those of control. And try to work out just whose benefit it's all for.

A final observation about the two Cs:

CASE HISTORY

Gillian was a newly qualified teacher. She was filled with wonderful idealism. A bit naive, but enthusiastic nevertheless. She would take her new class and lead them rather than push them. She would inspire them to learn. She would break down the oppressive barriers of school rules and liberate these fragile juvenile minds to the fascinating world of books and knowledge.

Silly Gillian. The first class they gave her was, of course, the toughest. They always do that to innocent young teachers. It's called the 'deep end' and Gillian was thrown into it. The school administration wanted to find out whether she was going to be educational wheat or chaff.

Gillian began her first lesson telling the little darlings that there would be no rules and that they were to call her by her first name. She was a lamb and the slaughter did not take long. Gillian was discharged from the clinic after only two weeks. By then she had decided to pursue a career in pottery and silk-screening.

The moral of this story? Control comes before care. You must set up the control mechanisms first. Then you can develop a more caring relationship. The drill sergeant makes it clear to the platoon that he is the boss. From day one. Then he can slowly mellow and reveal to this group of hardened soldiers that he, too, has a warm and fuzzy side. But only for a few seconds at a time.

If you set up the control dynamics before the care stuff comes in, then you set up *boundaries*. And that's what the next paradigm is all about.

PARADIGM 5

The boundary paradigm: me versus not-me

The question to be asked: Does this person have, and respect, boundaries?

This stuff is pretty nebulous but important to grasp. When you put this book down and go off people-watching you must observe how people respect or disrespect boundaries. So what are 'boundaries'? Some boundaries are physical, some are behavioural and others relate to identity. So what does all that mean? Read on.

EXERCISE

---

❶ Get into a lift with two or three people in it.
❷ Now stand far too close to someone in the lift.
❸ Watch them fidget. Observe their look of annoyance.
   Wait until they say something sharp and fractious to you.
   You've just crossed a physical boundary. We all observe

these, quite unconsciously, every day. We do not sit down beside a stranger at the beach. There are unspoken rules about doing some instantaneous geometrical calculations and leaving equal distances between you and everyone else around you.

❹ If the other person gets a kick out of it and starts to chat you up then you should leave the lift at the next floor. This exercise is not supposed to be a substitute for a dating service . . .

So those are physical boundaries. Now a look at boundaries of behaviour.

consider this

The magistrate is not amused. You're up for your seventh speeding fine. He gives you one of those long patronising speeches about your irresponsibility and how you are putting the public at risk by your incessant speeding, etc. You've crossed that boundary just once too often to hang on to your driver's licence.

now consider this

Gillian is back. She's given up pottery and silk-screening. Now she's your teacher and she's madder than ever. If you put even one little toe out of line she'll be down on you like a ton of Lego . . . But something in you is pleased by the change. Because she has shown you her strength and put up some limits on your behaviour you feel, well, *safe*. At last you know where you stand.

now consider this

You've just started at a new job. The interviews were murder, but you got there in the end. The final performance in this ceremony is to hand you your 'job description'. It is a document that sounds as if it was written by a lawyer. It tells you what will be expected of you. What you must do and what you don't need to worry about. It tells you whose backsides you kick and whose boots to look out for. It tells you how much money, holiday pay, sick leave, etc. that you can expect. There it is, in black and white, a heavily worded document that lays down the boundaries on your work, your authority, your responsibility and your entitlements. And all this before you even set foot inside the office.

So there are examples of boundaries that are both physical (the experiment in the lift) and behavioural (the law, school rules and job descriptions). From this you can deduce that lawyers spend a lot of their time defending clients who have crossed boundaries (criminal law) or trying to define and redefine boundaries between parties (civil law). And you thought that they all wore wigs and appeared on TV . . .

Those boundaries are pretty cut and dried. When it comes to understanding people the boundaries to understand are those of the body or self-identity.

And now consider this

You go to an acupuncturist. You weren't looking forward to this because you hate needles. He makes you look like a human pin-cushion. Of course you feel better. If you have gone to all that trouble then you would have to believe in his treatment.

There is something very powerful about watching the boundary of your own body being pierced by a long metal object. It evokes something very primitive within us: an animalistic belief that this is equated with injury. A part of our brain tells us that we must be bleeding and dying. It acts to ease the pain and initiate the healing process. It comes as no surprise that many people have funny ideas about needles. They faint when they have blood taken and they refuse to have injections of any sort. Too much like being impaled.

On the other hand, this process of piercing the boundaries of the body can have a strong placebo action. Many years ago, when I was studying tropical medicine in Papua New Guinea, it was quite common for the indigenous people to say 'Mi laik sut, dokta', which is Pidgin English for 'I would like a "shoot" (injection) please doctor'. Medicine that pierced the skin must surely be more powerful than medicine that you simply swallow.

CASE HISTORY
_____

Herbert and Ingrid were having an affair. He knew that her husband was at work and she knew that he was coming over for a bit of, well, what couples do when they're having an affair. He opened the front gate (first boundary) and walked to the front door (second boundary). She was there to greet him. She led him through the doorway (third boundary) into the living room. They stayed there for a few minutes but then this was just delaying what they both wanted. Their hormones were giving them hell. So she led him through the doorway (fourth boundary) into the bedroom. There they took off their clothes (fifth boundary). The sixth boundary was not so much crossed as penetrated. And I'm not talking about needles here . . .

The lesson to be learned: the boundaries in this case history were all physical. They were gates, doorways, physical space, clothes and then the body itself. Boundaries must be crossed by invitation only and with much mutual respect. That's why rape is so offensive.

John was a bouncy baby boy. His mother thought that he was the best thing since microwave ovens. Whenever he squawked she brought him this wonderful soft thing to drink from. A horn of plenty. Plenty of milk, that is. He didn't even have to get up to go to the toilet. She looked after everything for John. He was the centre of her world. When she held him in her arms he felt that she was his big human robot. His body melted into hers. A delightful merging of bodily boundaries. From a child's-eye viewpoint.

Eighteen years later John bought a large and dangerous motorcycle and he got that feeling once again. At high speed he and his motorcycle would act as one. His body would merge into it. No boundaries. Just a sense of power. Over his robot-mother and his death machine.

But John survived and went on to get a girlfriend called Karen. She was attracted to John because of the glistening chrome on his death machine. Unfortunately John came to utterly dominate Karen and to treat her like his robot-mother and his motorbike. She was yet another extension of him. He would tell her to jump and she would ask 'how high?'. She didn't breastfeed him but he often barked to her to get him a beer. She would answer his every whim. And I mean every.

This last blurring of boundaries is the most subtle but most common boundary problem that occurs with people. John has not matured from his childhood state of being given everything. So as an adult he crosses boundaries by expecting Karen to do everything that he wants. In some primitive part of John's *mind (most of his mind is primitive, but this is a really primitive bit) he feels that Karen is part of him; there to do his bidding. He feels entitled to cross boundaries.*

Karen, on the other hand, is so needy and dependent that she is continually looking to men to shore up her weak boundaries. She is like a bubble trying to attach to another bubble in the hope that this will stop both of them from popping. The jargon term for this is that she is 'merger-hungry'. She has no sense of her boundaries (to protect her) and he has no respect for boundaries anyway. What a pair . . .

PARADIGM 6

The order paradigm: order versus chaos

The question to be asked: How primitive are this person's defences?

Chaos theory is built around our new understanding that chaos and order are not distinct entities within nature. Pure order exists only within the minds of humans. We invented it and we bust our guts too strive for it. You will find order within the chaos that exists in nature (wave patterns, weather predictions, etc.) if you look deeply enough and with the right instruments.

What, I hear you ask, does chaos theory have to do with understanding people and their personalities? Bear with me a bit as I muse on the wonders of cosmology.

At this very moment all over the world astrophysical whizz-kids are studying the origins of the universe. What they have not paid much attention to is how the universe will end, but as that will be long after you and I have gone I don't think it's so bad to play ostrich.

Anyway, they believe that the world started with a Big Bang. A point in non-existent space that was of infinite density and infinite mass just up and exploded one day. And there, in all its far-flung beauty, is your universe. At that moment time and space came into being. There's no point in talking about what happened *before* the Big Bang since time didn't exist then. But don't sweat about that too much. It'll give you a headache.

The universe is heading to the state of greatest *entropy*. That means that it will end up with all matter as far as possible from all other matter and no flow of energy between any parts of the system. A vast, flat, unenergetic universe. Then the process will be reversed and everything will head back to that point where the Big Bang originated in a process that has been called, for obvious reasons, the Gnab Gib. This means that some of our distant descendants are going to be left with the ticklish problem of trying to fit all of humanity into a space much smaller than a pinhead. This is the way the world ends: not with a bang, but a hell of a crush.

Again I hear you ask, what has all this got to do with personalities?

In the midst of this gigantic ebb and flow exist you, me and the rest of humankind. We sit on this little planet and spend our days, like ants on the anthill that is called 'Earth', trying to create order out of chaos. We build, we refine, we educate. We hunger for knowledge. We try to improve upon everything that has ever been discovered or invented or understood previously.

We go to work where we try to either produce things (primary industry) or prop up and support all those who are busy producing (secondary industry). When we stay at home we form small communes called 'families' that are dedicated to the production and development of more human beings.

We in the West look with pity upon those in the Third World. We say that they have a primitive lifestyle and feel that we are advanced. But what are we advancing towards? And why are we motivated by such a powerful desire to create order from chaos when the universe itself is moving in exactly the opposite direction: the dissipation of energy and the distancing of all matter? We struggle to create order and the universe rushes into chaos.

There are some theologians who believe that humankind will become more and more sophisticated until we eventually merge into oneness with God. Of course we all know a lot of arrogant people who think they've made it already.

And now back to personalities. There is a microcosm of order and chaos that goes on in the mind of every human being. We are all trying to be more ordered. We use terms like sophistication, socialisation and maturity.

So how do you tell which people are sophisticated? By the labels on their clothing? By the plum in the mouth? By how much money, power, status or fame they have? No, no, no. Sophisticated people are not necessarily people with the most wealth or style or fame. On the contrary, *sophisticated people* are those who have *sophisticated defences*.

Defences are those little psychological processes that defend us from emotional pain. They help us keep our primitive, animalistic instincts in control. Defences help us to get on with other human beings in some sort of socialised way.

consider this

You have a flat tyre. It went with a bang. Not such a big deal except that you're in the middle of the world's biggest traffic jam and it's rush hour. You end up on the side of the highway. You're wearing your best business clothes and you know that they're going to end up covered in grease. Then you open the boot of your car and find that your spare is flat. So what do you do? You laugh. You laugh until you cry. A sophisticated defence. Better than bashing the smithereens out of your useless car.

now consider this

At one of those cocktail parties with the skites and the over-imbibers, you're itching to find someone to mention 'chaology' to. You encounter an obnoxious woman who wants to challenge everything that you hold near and dear. You're male so she wants to blame you for every crime ever committed by any man against any woman. You're in business so she spends some time educating you about the evils of capitalism. Eventually she extracts from you that you voted for party 'X' in the last election. Big mistake. The onslaught continues. You find yourself fantasising about breaking a champagne bottle against her head and launching her down the front steps. But you keep your cool and keep intellectualising with her. How sophisticated!

now consider this

You're a hopeless drunk. People confront you with it. You continually deny it. Denial is such an unsophisticated defence. One day you wake up in the gutter with vomit all over you. You continue to deny that you're an alcoholic and go looking for the next drink. Primitive defences often hang around like this.

You're a kid playing in the school playground. The teacher nabs you for something. You swear black and blue that someone else did it. It's called *projection*. It's an unsophisticated defence that disowns anything bad or anti-social. You claim only the good stuff.

Later in life you continue the blame game. Whichever government is in power. Your neighbours. Everyone is doing wrong by you. And you're never wrong.

A convenient defence mechanism. But inflexible. And primitive.

So the moral of Paradigm 6 is that we human beings are trying to create order out of a universe that is hurtling towards greater chaos. Some people help us forward. They are sophisticated people with sophisticated defences. Others hold us back. They have unsophisticated defences. And they're Painful People *par excellence*.

PARADIGM 7

The Love paradigm: passion versus security

In your people-watching, nothing will reveal more about a person than the way they love other people. Painful People usually have a big love problem. A need for it. A refusal of it. Too much self-love.

Or not enough. Unsuccessful relationships are the hallmark of the Painful Person.

There's something about love. We hanker after it. We read books and watch movies that have as their central theme a love relationship of some form or other. It's supposed to make the world go round. But *what is it?*

Perhaps you should ask *'what are they?'* What are the ways of loving? There seems to be more than one concept that we refer to with this little four-letter word.

EXERCISE

---

❶ Sit through a night of television. Drink lots of coffee if you must. I agree that most of it is doggerel.

❷ Don't watch the shows, just the advertisements. That seems to be most of the time on air. Someone trying to sell you this product or that service.

❸ Now divide all the advertisements that you have seen into two groups. The first group is for the ads that portrayed the product as being new, modern, super-duper, technological and space-age. The second group is for the ads that displayed the product as being old, tried, true, tested, proven, genuine and smelling of leather and cigars.

❹ Now try to find an ad that doesn't fit into either category. There aren't any.

So it is with love. It is either:

♦ young, hormonal, erotic, poetic, occurring in spring and associated with your heart skipping a beat when they walk into the room, or

♦ old, secure, trusting, mutually dependable, perennial and comfortable as a pair of old slippers.

The first is what I call 'heart–genital' love and the second is what I call 'head–stomach' love. Just like in the ads.

Heart–genital love is easy. Head–stomach love is hard. Heart–genital love comes first, unless you're getting yourself into an arranged marriage. Head–stomach love comes later, when the two of you have settled into a plodding and secure relationship. But if you ever lose the ability to kick a bit of heart–genital love back into your relationship then it becomes stale, bored and mundane.

CASE HISTORY

Lorraine met Mark in a bar. She had her mask on: make-up, mascara, ruby-red lipstick. Her pretty painted face screamed 'come and try your luck, suckers'. She was out for a night on the town.

Some jerks came and tried to chat her up. She didn't say many words to them. The ones she did say were sweet but firm. They said 'push off, hairylegs'. The jerks pushed off.

Then she clapped eyes on Mark. In the 'meat market' there are all sorts of unspoken rules. The agenda is decided before the first word is uttered. Lorraine sized up Mark. Mark sized up Lorraine. Lorraine then pushed her hair back, did something cute with her lips and fluttered her eyelids at him, just a teensy bit. Mark smiled a debonair smile at her. But he was resisting the temptation to shout a jubilant 'Yes!'. All this had occurred from across the room, but with a bit of animalistic displaying both Lorraine and Mark had set the agenda. Some time tonight they would cross all six boundaries in about four minutes flat.

There followed all the preening and courtship. You don't read these in any books. People in the meat market just sort of know.

It is a game. For men it is called 'the pursuit and conquest'. Women who are good at it refer to it in more vulgar terms: 'follow me, f*** me'. There is a lot of playing hard to get and seeming disinterested. That's a power play and is supposed to make you look cool at a time when you're feeling really, really hot. At some time in the evening there is a decision to be made about 'whose place'. Then in the privacy of a bedroom a primitive ritual is carried out. For men it is associated with fantasies of being a sexual magnet that no woman can resist. For women it is called 'sweet surrender'. Heart–genital love triumphs again.

But then Lorraine and Mark run into a problem. In the morning the game is over. Her mask has worn off. He looks a bit pale and puny in the harsh morning sun. Both of them have a headache and a case of the dry horrors. Back again in the cold, clammy grip of reality the couple part with promises that they will get together again. They never do; neither ever intended to. This was not a game of finding your lifetime partner. This was a bonk.

But in their hearts they keep looking. For more and more people to bolster their fragile sexual egos; to make them feel attractive; to make them feel loved and lovable, even if it is for an erotic oasis in the desert of their lives.

There is a pattern to heart–genital love. It follows the same course:

Step 1: encounter
Step 2: attraction
Step 3: fantasy
Step 4: seduction
Step 5: idealisation

Step 6: disappointment
Step 7: disillusionment
Step 8: anger
Step 9: rejection
Step 10: now go back to step 1 . . .

All over the world people enact this cycle again and again. What they don't know is that they're not really looking for bigger and better orgasms. They're looking for head–stomach love.

C A S E   H I S T O R Y

Norma and Oscar met at work. They worked in the same office. There was a mutual attraction early on. They could establish this without having to play too many hair-stroking and seduction games. They just felt comfortable in each other's presence. They respected the quality of each other's work. They had some things in common, like their culture, their intelligence and their sense of humour. And they had things that were different. When one was falling apart with the stresses of the job the other one could comfort and soothe. Perfect yin and yang. They were soulmates.

One day Oscar and Norma were chatting over the water cooler. They tended to linger there. Flirting, I suppose. He plucked up enough courage to ask Norma out. This was very traditional. His making the first move.

He had thought long and hard about it. What if she said 'no'? What if they began a relationship and it didn't work out?

He was delighted when she responded positively. They never looked back. Sure there was lots of game-playing and seduction and the odd dirty weekend that they both made really, really dirty. But they were safe with each other. Not too many power plays and plenty of good communication, even about the painful issues.

She moved in with him. Then a year or two later they got married. By this time the hormonal stuff was starting to die down. But that was okay because they knew all of each other's annoying little habits. And they had had some huge fights and survived them with some mutual forgiveness. Heart–genital love was becoming head–stomach love. The more they worked on it the better they got.

Development of a relationship

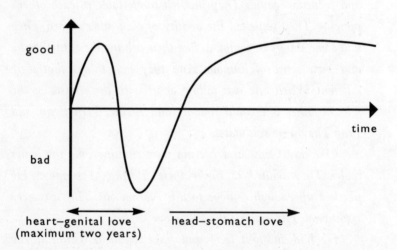

So did Norma and Oscar live happily ever after? Get real. This is no fairy story. Norma and Oscar went through some pretty tedious times in their marriage. Her post-natal

depression and his redundancy. His mid-life crisis and her menopause. Sometimes they felt like putting ground glass into the other's breakfast cereal. Then they would get away from the kids and have one of those dirty weekends together. A sweet blend of heart–genital and head–stomach love.

They survived. Marriage is like that. A mature ability to love and be loved. Hard work at times but worth it.

Such is love. And I describe it because truly Painful People can never get it right. They either avoid it or move from intense, transient unstable relationship to intense, transient unstable relationship. Or hang onto a bad relationship for too long. They just never quite get it right.

PARADIGM 8

The insight paradigm: content versus process

The question to be asked: What is the *process* that exists beneath the *content* of this person's behaviour?

Understanding people is all about getting the big picture. It is about spotting the agenda. Reading between the lines. Getting beyond what is spoken, enacted, presented. At the risk of sounding a little paranoid, when it comes to people-watching all is not as it may seem.

Insight is about cutting through swathes of *content* and into the *process*.

When Lorraine and Mark were eyeing each other in the bar the content was mutual inspection. The process was seduction. When Norma and Oscar were working out how to grind up the glass the content was planning a murder. The process was a problem in their marriage that was making one or other so frustrated that they were sitting on murderous rage.

consider this

Your boss is always checking up on you. He seems to be always looking over your shoulder. He closely inspects everything that you produce even though he never finds a mistake. He expects you to report to him ten times a day. When he goes away on holiday he phones in every day to find out 'how things are going'.
Content: an intrusive, controlling boss.
Process: a boss with a personality problem. He cannot show respect to his staff by trusting them to come up with the goods. In fact he has a lot of problems with trust. His wife left him last year because of his infernal jealousy. He has an obsessional streak. He has a fear of authority (those above him in the corporate hierarchy) and anxiety that they will attack his department. See? Lots of process stuff. All you've got to do is look for it.

now consider this

Your best friend at work breaks down and cries. She pulls herself together quickly and tries to pretend that it hasn't happened. You go to comfort her. She is a bit edgy and doesn't want to talk about it. Not too long after that she goes away on a long 'holiday'.

Content: some tears and a vacation.
Process: previously undiagnosed depression.

now consider this

Your previously plump teenage niece suddenly and inexplicably loses a lot of weight while at the same time becoming fairly obsessive about cooking and taking on the role of feeding the family. When you surreptitiously ask her about her weight loss she looks at you with a facile, wide-eyed smile and tries to give the impression that she doesn't know what you're talking about.
Content: a young woman losing weight in order to be slim and attractive.
Process: a young woman who may be becoming anorexic.

now consider this

Your teenage son becomes even more bumptious than ever before. He is provocative and self-centred. He is slovenly and has more body odour than you can handle. He starts failing at school. He changes his peer group from a mildly obnoxious group of adolescents for a severely obnoxious gang of thugs. He keeps wanting to 'borrow' money but doesn't seem to have anything to show for it. He used to be a pretty decent kid. Now he's getting harder and harder to love.
Content: Adolescent turmoil.
Process: The kid's in trouble. Is he depressed? Dabbling in drugs? Time for a heart-to-heart with junior, if he'll let you get that close.

now consider this

Your nine-year-old daughter comes to you one morning and says that she aches all over. She looks pretty healthy to you but you're a 'soft touch' and let her have a day off school. It comes as no surprise that her physical condition improves dramatically after 9 a.m.

Content: A child's report of her symptoms.

Process: A classical 'sicky'. So why doesn't she want to go to school? Because there's a new kid in the class who is picking on her, that's why. And a deeper process behind that: the new kid's need to be noticed and accepted into a peer group, thereby displacing your daughter. And deeper still: the new kid's insecurity caused by the instability of her life since her mother keeps getting and losing boyfriends. Want to go any deeper?

now consider this

The old woman who lives next door has just been diagnosed with cancer. She was always a strong and fiercely independent character. She tells you with some pride and fortitude that she's going to 'beat this thing'. She embarks on a treatment that combines everything orthodox with anything else she can get her hands on. She does the chemotherapy, the acupuncture, the prune juice, the osteopathy and a lot of praying.

Content: a woman who is determined to win.

Process: a woman who is terrified of dying.

and now consider this

The salesman wants to sell you product X. He approaches you in a gentle way. He seems keen to know how he can help you. He talks of doing an analysis of your needs. That impresses you. As does the follow-up phone call that he makes.

Content: a salesman who wants to help you.

Process: a salesman who wants your money. He just learned those soft-sell techniques at salesman school.

So, people-watchers, all may not be as it seems. Painful — and Pain-full — People often use these subterfuges. Like doing a favour so that you will be indebted to them. Like telling you something private about themselves as a way of getting you to spill the beans about yourself. Power plays. Layers upon layers of process beneath the superficial veneer of content. But if you can't see the big picture you'll get sucked in.

PARADIGM 9

The system paradigm: individual versus systemic

> The question to be asked: To what systems does this person belong?

When you're sniffing out all those Painful People it's important to keep in mind their system. I mean their family, company, team, tribe or parish. The human animal is very social: we naturally huddle together in masses. Safety in numbers I suppose. And Painful People can impinge upon a human group in a number of ways. They can be painful because of the group, like a cult member. Or they can lead a group, like Dennis the control-freak. Or they can destroy a group because of their ability to sabotage the plans of others. That's why they're painful. Don't say I didn't warn you.

Peter was not so much painful as pain-full. His father didn't hang around for his birth. In fact he hung around long enough to cross the six boundaries and then split.

Nevertheless Peter took his father's surname. When his mother shacked up with one of her boyfriends it caused him some distress that they each had a different name. He envied the kids at school whose siblings and parents were all Smiths or Joneses. He wanted to belong.

His mother's relationship didn't last. None of them did. She was a good-hearted woman who had a steely strength in times of adversity. But she chose all the wrong men. Cheats, liars, manipulators, nutters. They sort of drifted into Peter's life, hung around long enough for him to get to know them and then they drifted out again. Some of them were nice. Incompetent at maintaining an intimate relationship, but still nice in that painful sort of way.

Peter became sensitised to loss. People can stand only so much abandonment before they make an unconscious decision to never let anyone get close again. He yearned for a conventional middle-class family with a house with a picket fence and a father who'd come and watch him play football.

But what he grew up with was the classical disengaged *family. They're families where there is no firm sense of* boundaries. *It's a bit hard to work out where the family begins and ends. Members don't share the same name. People just drift in and out. There is no initiation ceremony (marriage, christening) and no sense of leadership. When*

*people want to go, all they have to do is pack their bags.
Like Peter's many step-fathers.*

The opposite to the *disengaged* family is the enmeshed one. Like
Rosemary's . . .

C A S E   H I S T O R Y
_____

*Rosemary's father was captain of the family ship. No one
questioned his orders. Much of Rosemary's mother's time was
spent in soothing her father's fragility. If he didn't get his way
there was hell to pay.*

    *But at least there was a strong sense of family. Picket
fences and private schools, just like those Peter dreamed of. Yet
behind the pleasantness of the suburban ideal was a private
hell. No love. Nothing relaxed or warm. Just mind-control.
Like a family-sized cult. Father's opinion became family policy.
Not to be questioned. Or face the consequences of guilt and
shame until you repented.*

    *No one entered or left this family without father's say-so. In
particular his children would need his explicit approval if they
were to make any big decisions in life, such as leaving home or
getting married. Rosemary knew that when she and her siblings
married, their spouses would never truly be part of the family.
Just hangers-on. Rigid boundaries. Too rigid. Not enough letting
go of power by the old man. He would grasp it until he died.
And then his children would bury him with a combined sense of
grief and liberation. Your classical enmeshed family.*

The family is the prototype of all subsequent human systems.
Sigmund Freud said that. He got it right. Just look at every human
system. They all start to look the same: boundaries, hierarchies,

leadership, traditions, commonly held beliefs and policies, rules and discipline, an established way of information being passed around the system and, above all, roles.

So disengagement and enmeshment are processes that occur in corporations, bikie gangs and bowling clubs. People in business suits have been studying family dynamics for decades without realising it. They call it 'management'.

When your Painful People detector indicates that you have found a well-and-truly painful person, just check out their systems. There'll be something tragic going on there. Bet on it.

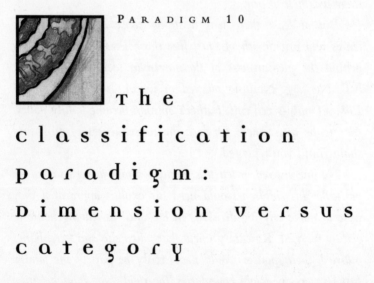

PARADIGM 10

The classification paradigm: Dimension versus category

The question to be asked: How can this person's personality be categorised?

Paradigms, like commandments, come in groups of ten. So here's the last. It's possibly the most important. It addresses this question: personalities are such complex things, so how do you classify them? If we are all a bit painful and all a bit pain-full then what makes us different from each other?

There are two ways to classify personalities: they are called dimension and category. Psychologists do more of the former and psychiatrists do more of the latter.

First, dimensions. This means that you take a person's personality and break it into a variety of characteristics or traits. You might be high on cunning and low on flexibility. Low on intelligence and high on brute strength, etc. An individual then becomes a series of numbers on a psychologist's report and the captains of industry are well pleased.

This is like taking all cars on the road and breaking them down into dimensions, such as their colour, automatic versus manual, with or without power steering, motor less than or greater than two litres, etc., etc. You could then reduce every car to a series of numbers. But why?

Reducing any entity to a series of traits pleases the analytical and reductionist amongst us. But most of us think of personalities as categories.

EXERCISE

❶ Go down to your local New Age bookshop. You know, the ones with the incense wafting out the door, the sound of whale calls from within and all the crystals in the display window.

❷ Buy a book on astrology. Star signs and stuff. Even if you don't believe in it, it's still worth reading. Single people like Lorraine and Mark who hang around in bars use this baloney as a way to start the chat-up. ('So you're an Aquarius! My third husband was an Aquarius too!')

❸ Now get a neutral second party to read out from the book the account of what sort of personality style each type of star sign is supposed to be. This is a fine example of how personalities are *categorised*. A whole lot of traits clumped together in one category.

❹ Now try to guess which of those personalities belongs to your star sign. You'll have exactly one chance in twelve of getting it right . . .

❺ Now go back to the New Age shop and demand your money back. Watch the girl with the dangly ear-rings and the gypsy scarf on her head get flustered. See her point at the sign saying 'no refunds'. Relent now. Say you'll swap it for a pack of Tarot cards. Watch her sigh of relief. After all she's only working here part-time while she does her doctorate in quantum physics.

❻ Now look at the Tarot cards. More categories. *Archetypes* in fact. Jung would be proud of you. There are people who are categorised as the royal figures, peasants, executioners and, of course, the Tarot equivalent of the Grim Reaper. This is the next step beyond categorisation. You and I don't have to get as esoteric as that.

As you plough through the descriptions of Painful People in the ensuing pages you'll find that I rely heavily on this process of categorisation. Once you get the hang of it you'll find that these categories are like beauty and ugliness: *they are easy to recognise but difficult to define.*

There is, of course, a major drawback with categorising: what about the people who don't fit the categories? What about the person who is a little bit of most of them and a whole lot of the rest? What about the person for whom there is no easy pigeon-hole? Good question. And one for which I have no glib answer. Except that it must be kept in mind that categories are simply a tool. Don't expect to find everyone you know and hate to be described in these categories. But then again don't be surprised if you do . . .

Before we get categorising, let me inform you of the most basic category of all. When I encounter a new patient in my practice and I am trying to draw a bead on their personality I ask myself two questions. These are basic. They relate to whether and how this person can tolerate *intimacy*. Because most Painful People show just how painful they can be within the context of a relationship.

personality styles

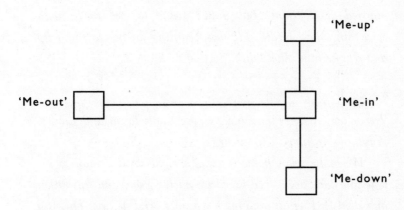

Question one is 'Does this person strive to achieve *intimate* relationships?' Note the emphasis on *intimate*. I'm not just looking at how they get on with their neighbours or workmates. People's warts and foibles, all of their strengths and weaknesses, are revealed in an intimate relationship, one in which there is emotion and need involved. We can all put on a mask when we are relating to people who are emotionally unimportant to us. But when we really want and need someone then the stakes are much higher. Just look at how people manage anger within their relationships . . .

CASE HISTORY

Sarah was a successful business executive. At work she was into power dressing, power talking, power breathing, power full stop.

She was assertive and confident. No one dare give Sarah any grief or they would live to rue the day.

But when Sarah came home she was a doormat to her husband. She was terrified of disappointing him. She needed him and she would please him so that he would never go away. Yet why did he continue to treat her with such contempt? Because he had fallen in love with a business executive and married a doormat. He didn't want to get away with everything that he did. He was yearning for her to stand up and rebuke him. She didn't. So that's why he left her.

CASE HISTORY

Trevor was a sop. He would be obsequious to all and sundry. Anything to curry their favour.

When he went home he was a right royal demon to his wife and kids. As if he'd saved up all his anger and frustration and then let it erupt onto his loved ones. And he had. This is a process called displacement. He should have dumped all this anger on his boss and customers. But he dumped it on his family instead. He felt that this was safe: they would never leave him because they needed him.

They didn't (need him) and they did (leave him).

So back to question one: 'Does this person strive to achieve intimate relationships?' If they do, then I call them 'Me-in' people. If they don't they're 'Me-out' people. For obvious reasons.

Now for question two: 'If this person strives to achieve intimate relationships, do they habitually adopt a dominant or a submissive role within these relationships?' It comes as no surprise that I call them 'Me-up' and 'Me-down' people. No prize for guessing which is which.

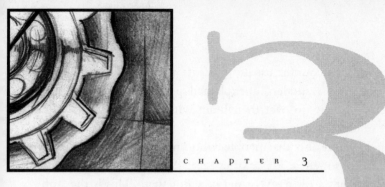

CHAPTER 3

SO WHAT'S A PERSONALITY?

Hard thing to define, personality. It seems to have something to do with how you *get on with life*: getting on with people, getting on with accomplishing things, getting on with living. It's unique to you, just like your fingerprint, and it starts to show in a solid form from late adolescence.

To define it further, let's start with your God-given gifts. Things like intelligence, talent, creativity, etc. Now add some other component: how much zest and energy you put into it all, i.e. mood and motivation. Now add the all-important ingredient: a habitual style of relating. Once again the old theme: the best and worst aspects of a person's personality are revealed within their relationships.

Now mix the ingredients in a bowl greased with DNA and there you have it: you. Or at least your personality.

Sometimes personality changes as you grow. It usually does this as a slow, mellowing process. This is why psychotherapists often take their time with patients. The only good changes are slow ones. The sudden personality changes associated with an intense conversion or encounter usually dissipate just as suddenly. And if people undergo a sudden, unexplained personality change then we doctors usually go over their brain with a fine-toothed comb trying to find something *organic*.

Keep in mind also that people who are really nasty or nerdy also tend to soften a bit as they age. Although there's *always* something that's a bit nasty or nerdy about them. This is the stuff of silk purses and sow's ears.

Now take on board three important dynamics that I'll describe below. They are models of dysfunctional couples, dysfunctional families and what to do when you are in a pickle. They are called the *Spanner Theory*, the *Z-phenomenon* and the *three Cs*.

THE SPANNER THEORY

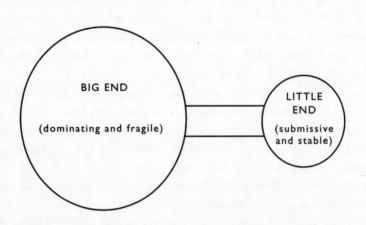

This is about couples. It's my own way of describing a style of relating that has come to be called 'co-dependence'. That is a term that I particularly dislike because it so damned Californian. And it would lead you to believe that it's not a good idea to be dependent. Hogwash! We're all dependent. The trick in life is to balance our need to be dependent against our need to be autonomous. Now there's a juggling act if I ever saw one . . .

It's called the Spanner Theory because it's got a Big End and a Little End. If spanners have ends that are the same size their usefulness is reduced by exactly fifty per cent. Think about it.

The Big End is a person who is *dominating and fragile*. The Little End is a person who is *submissive and stable*. Two thirds of the time the Big End is the man. The other third of the time the Big End is the woman. In this latter case she is married to that wretch who is called the 'hen-pecked husband'.

Big Ends *control* Little Ends. They do this by one of three ways: intimidation, seduction or guilt. Intimidation gives the message that 'if you do not do what I want, bad things will happen to you'. Seduction gives the message that 'if you do what I want, good things will happen to you'. Guilt is just guilt. The message here is 'you are responsible for my happiness (or unhappiness)'.

Little Ends *care for* Big Ends. See the pattern emerging here? Little Ends want to give, love, care and rescue. They readily take responsibility for the happiness of their Big End. And if you can get into the mind of a Big End you find that they look upon their Little Ends as an extension of themselves. She is the outrigger of his canoe, the counter-weight of his pendulum. The Boundary Paradigm is alive and well and living in this style of relationship.

Big Ends are Me-up people; Little Ends are Me-down people. Big Ends have a fear of intimacy and Little Ends have a fear of abandonment. Or at least that's how it seems. Until it falls apart. And it usually does.

You see, Big Ends can slowly destroy their Little Ends. They do this by *projecting* upon them. Little Ends are continually exposed to the message 'I'm good, right and holy. You're bad, wrong and sinful'. When this projection is combined with some self-protective rationalising then it becomes a phenomenon called CRAP. That stands for Confident Rationalisation And Projection. Big Ends are full of it.

This message gradually chips away at the Little End's self-esteem. Eventually she does one or more of three things: she gets depressed, or she gets angry or she gets out. Usually she does all three, and in that exact order. Her depression is about not having her own emotional needs met in the marriage. When she realises that, she gets angry. Then she goes. Men often threaten to abandon their women as a weapon. But they never go. Of if they do, they go for a week and then come back. When a woman goes, *she's gone*. When a woman decides that a marriage is over, *it's over*.

When Little Ends do their three things then it's time for the Big Ends to do *their* three things. They have to (1) get her back or (2) replace her or (3) fall apart. We men usually don't realise how dependent we are until our women leave us. That's when great big hairy macho men start to weep and panic. Not a pretty sight.

So why, I hear you ask, do Little Ends get involved in these destructive relationships? The answer is that Little Ends are either compulsive mothers or compulsive daughters. Compulsive daughters are attracted to the tough, controlling exterior of Big Ends but mistake this for protection. Women carry a vulnerability with them for as long as they live. They are physically smaller than men and continually aware of the risk of sexual assault. They want to relate to a man with whom they can walk down a dark alley. So when they encounter this controlling man they find that he has a fatal attraction for them. What they have yet to learn is that his control is purely egocentric.

Compulsive mothers are Little Ends who recognise that within their Big End exists a little hurting boy who needs to be soothed. Some Big Ends exploit this from time to time. Just as their Little Ends are ready to murder them or leave them, the Big Ends will do something very endearing or they will reveal their inner vulnerability. This seduces the Little End to come rushing back to rescue them. But she'll only do this about a thousand times before she cottons on to what's happening here . . .

And that's the Spanner Theory. Now that you know what it is you'll see it everywhere. When it comes to power-sharing no couple ever gets it *completely* right.

THE Z - PHENOMENON

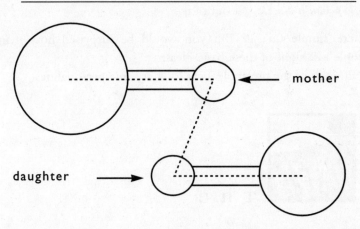

The Z-Phenomenon is a variation of the Spanner Theory theme. It involves a Big End who is male, emotionally incompetent and distanced from his Little End. Her emotional needs are not being met within the marriage. So she develops an enmeshed relationship with one of her children, usually a daughter. The daughter ends up 'mothering' mother. Not a good role for a kid who finds that she, in turn, is missing out emotionally.

When she grows up she's attracted to men whom she can 'mother' like this because that's the only way that she can relate to others. So she chooses Big Ends. Hence the 'Z' in the diagram above. And the cycle goes on. And on. And on . . .

And that's the Z-Phenomenon.

This one is quite straightforward. Bear it in mind when you find yourself in a situation that is intolerable. This might be at work or in an intimate relationship. The three Cs are your options. And there are only three of them. They are:

- *Cope*, i.e. put up with it.
- *Change*, i.e. make it better.
- *Cut'n'run*, i.e. get out of it.

There, simple isn't it? But you would be surprised how many people lose sight of these basic ideas.

Enough of the preamble. Let's look at some personalities.

 # The Narcissist

If you're looking for an example of a Big End, you've just found one.

CASE HISTORY

Terry was a bloke who seemed to have no doubts about his own self-worth. He was, to coin a phrase, up himself. He thought that he was God's gift to the world. At the saying of his name, all knees should bend. Terry was so far up himself that one day he went to a revolving restaurant and exalted in the fantasy that all the world was revolving around him.

You can imagine what a painful person he was. He thought that he was so, well, special. He would boast until everyone around him was nearly asleep with boredom. He didn't walk, he sort of strutted. And he would always tell you about some grand scheme that was going to make him a millionaire.

He couldn't walk past a mirror without preening himself. He seemed to need continual admiration so he surrounded himself with a few friends who would agree with anything he said.

If Terry was ever criticised his reaction was a sight to behold. He would fall to pieces in a screaming, abusive heap. In the process he would make a complete ass of himself. The more he did it the more out of control he became. What he was revealing was his fragility. He was like a sheet of glass. When he cracked he did it in a big way. And after this he would brood and fester like a piqued little boy. Then, slowly, he would re-assemble himself and get on with his haughty strutting through life.

Another feature of Terry's personality was his ability to be manipulative. He would exploit people in any way he could. And he seemed to have no ability to experience true compassion. No ability to empathise. He was utterly self-centred. A true Big End. And a pathetic individual if he were not so painful.

COMMENT

Narcissists are named after Narcissus, the beautiful young man of Greek mythology who looked into a pond, saw his own reflection for the first time and promptly fell in love with himself. Just like Terry preening himself in front of mirrors.

This is the Narcissist in all his self-concocted glory. The characteristics are:

♦ his arrogance and his need for continual applause and admiration
♦ the way he uses people and doesn't seem to give a damn about it
♦ the fragility of his self-esteem. He comes across as being haughty but this is often an over-compensation for very profound feelings of inadequacy. When they begin to feel inadequate they decompensate into *narcissistic rage*. So what's that?

consider this

You're painting a wall. You spill some paint on the carpet. You mutter a curse under your breath and tell yourself that you should've used those bloody drop sheets like so-and-so told you. You pause to recompose yourself. You're frustrated but you count to ten and it passes. You know that you'll struggle later to try to get the paint out of the carpet, fail miserably and then get some expensive professional carpet cleaner in grey overalls to come in and charge you an arm and a leg to get the paint out of the carpet.

That's normal anger.

now consider this

You're painting a wall. You spill some paint on the carpet. You fly into a rage. You make growling sounds behind your clenched teeth. You splash paint angrily all over the wall so that even more of it goes onto the carpet. Then you pound your paintbrush against the wall so that you bend the bristles. Then you slump into a sullen heap and brood about the bloody paint for the rest of the day.

Your anger is inordinate, destructive and persistent. Now *that's* narcissistic rage.

Narcissists are mostly men. (Some adolescents come across as being very narcissistic. If they do, give them a few years and they might grow out of it.) A recent study also showed that these men can mellow if one of three things happens to them:

- ♦ they do extremely well in life. This results in the feeling of their own importance finally matching up with the way that people regard them. For the Terrys of this world it relieves them of the torment they experience when they need applause and don't get it.
- ♦ they do extremely badly in life. Paradoxical isn't it? But if a narcissist is a flop at work or in relationships then it's actually quite healthy for him. It knocks the edges off his arrogance and puts his feet on the ground. A pain-full process but it stops him from being so painful.
- ♦ they develop a stable, ongoing relationship. Usually with someone who tells them when to get off. If a narcissist's partner can knock him into shape then he feels 'contained'. Within the heart of the Narcissist is a yearning to find someone who is stronger than him.

What sort of childhood do narcissists have? Often they have a parent who dotes on them too much. Narcissists grow up with the message that they truly are exceptional. Then they hit that school of hard knocks called 'adulthood', where they're told that they're not. They keep trying to remind the world that they're special. And the world disagrees.

Terry is a rather extreme example of a narcissist. But research shows that at any one time about five per cent of men will show some fairly significant and annoying narcissistic traits. Now that's a scary statistic. I weep for my gender . . .

And now the final paradox: as I stated in the Pathology Paradigm, *it's all a matter of degree*. People who don't have *any* narcissistic traits usually become too self-effacing, too compassionate and not ambitious enough. We must all carry a bit of Narcissus within us. It gives us some drive and ruthlessness when necessary. If you don't have any of this, you get nowhere in life.

Put up with them as much as you can. That's a good start. Don't marry one unless you can contain their need to feel 'special' by continually reminding them that they're not. Keep in mind that the Narcissist is yearning to find someone who will keep him in check, resist his demands and give him a realistic appraisal of his worth. When a narcissist falls about in a rage, ignore him until he's prepared to act more respectably.

If all else fails, just hang in there. Narcissists go through *huge* mid-life crises when they have to come to terms with the fact that they're not youthful, attractive and agile any more. Then they mellow. A bit.

The Limpet

Limpets are mostly women. The essential feature of the Limpet is her ability to stick to a relationship even if it is destroying her.

EXERCISE

❶ Go down to the beach.
❷ Find a limpet attached to a rock.
❸ Try to prise it off. Kick it. Pull it. Beg it to let go. Promise it things. Like a bigger, better, smoother rock. Then go

home knowing that you're a lot more frazzled than the limpet is.

❹ Now you know why they're called Limpets.

C A S E   H I S T O R Y

Ursula clung. Mostly to men. She seemed to be desperately unhappy when she was not in a relationship and just as unhappy when she was. She chose all the wrong men. Bossy types. Big Ends. And then she became a Little End. Again and again and again.

She had no confidence in her own judgement. She continually sought out people who would reassure and encourage her. Or take responsibility for her.

She had a deep fear of being abandoned. She would do anything she could to please the man in her life. She would get him into bed on the first date and then put on her 'I'm a siren, you're a conqueror' routine in the hope that they would come back for more. Which they usually did. She was a pretty good siren . . .

The problem was that they wouldn't stay. Eventually they tired of her sense of inadequacy and her dependence and then they would leave. What Ursula didn't know was that these men were looking for a woman who had more strength and self-confidence. So Ursula got really good at limpeting herself onto someone on the rebound. Just about anyone would do. As long as she wasn't alone.

Ursula had a deep fear that she spoke of to no one. She was afraid that her parents would die. Given that they were thirty-odd years older than her the likelihood of her outliving them was on the high side. But they were the only constant things in her life. Constantly supportive too.

Eventually she hatched the idea that all she had to do was to get pregnant. Then she would have someone to love who would never leave her. Somewhere in her heart she admitted to herself that she really wanted to have a child so that her child could love her. Another 'Z-Phenomenon' in the making.

COMMENT

Need I say more? The characteristics of the Limpet are:

- ♦ her excessive dependence: she goes through life trying to find someone who will take care of her
- ♦ she'll do anything to hang on, even to the point of giving up her rights, her entitlements and her dignity
- ♦ she dreads being rejected or abandoned.

This is the truly dependent personality. But I've already done a song and dance about how *we're all dependent* and people are limpets only if they are really, really, stupidly, destructively dependent.

So what makes a person become a limpet? We psychiatrists just love to live in the past. Why? Because what happens in our past determines a lot of what will happen in our present and our future. And we like to beat up on parents. They're to blame for all the ills of the world. Right? Wrong.

Most parents, like most people, simply struggle through life. We all strive to be good-enough people, good-enough parents and good-enough partners. After all, no one's perfect. Right? You bet.

Having said that, be aware that sometimes parents do stuff it up badly. When it comes to caring for your children there are three ways you can go wrong:

◆ Give them too much care. Believe it or not that stops kids from individuating from their parents so they can't find their own ways of dealing with the 'hard knocks'. You'll end up with a Terry on your hands.

◆ Give them no care. No kids survive this unscathed. The worst become psychopaths. You've got a few more pages of reading before you get to this painful person.

◆ Give them care but make it really unreliable. Give it, then take it away. Be present, then be absent. Be loving then cruel. Keep your kids forever guessing where the next hug will come from. Inconsistency: a great way of breeding a limpet.

And another thing. Ursula was far too dependent. But don't lose sight of the notion that we're all dependent. You'll get sick of hearing this soon: *it's all a matter of degree.*

HOW TO DEAL WITH THE LIMPET

Limpets have to learn to be autonomous. Because they've usually had parental love that was thermostatic (on again, off again) they find it hard to *trust* people to stick around. They are just waiting for the next rejection.

Limpets have to work on themselves. The goal is to be more autonomous. Not completely independent (no one is) but more able to exist reasonably well when they are not in a relationship. That way when the next relationship starts they will go into it because they *want* to be there, not because they *have* to be there.

This is the sort of thing that is often handled in psychotherapy. The temptation there is for the Limpet to become too dependent on her therapist. Sometimes the most important part of a therapy like this is the letting go and the saying goodbye.

If you have a limpet as a partner then there are some challenges that you have:

♦ First you must gain her trust. Don't even start to do this if you don't intend to stick around. Nothing would be more destructive than her beginning to trust you and then you up and go. You want to give her the message that your relationship is safe. Or safe enough. No relationship lasts forever, even if it ends with one of you being put into a wooden box. But try to convince her that you won't abandon her.

♦ Now encourage her to work on herself. To have things that are hers. That she's responsible for. Like *her* job and *her* interests. And perhaps *her* psychotherapy. It's all about developing her own boundaries and a sense of her own identity.

 The Loner

Human beings just love to hang around other human beings. We yearn to hold a hand or be slapped on the back. We yearn to be touched. But not the Loner.

He is notable because he is so 'Me-out'. He shuns people. He can be as severe as an autistic or a hermit or as subtle as someone who is socially charming but always lives alone. Like no other group, Loners are truly pain-full. The group is heterogeneous so I'll describe a variety of 'cases' from the most to the least impaired.

Warren's mother knew that there was something wrong with her baby within the first few months. Warren was her third child so she knew that kids are supposed to watch their mother's gaze, smile, coo, explore, babble. All those cute baby-cum-toddler things. Warren did none of them. As Warren grew his mother would try to voice her concerns to her husband. He just smiled in a patronising way and gave her some reassurance that she ignored. There was something wrong with this kid.

Their GP was pretty switched on. She suspected the diagnosis from the moment she heard the story. No, Warren was not deaf or blind. Or retarded. He just avoided any social cues of any kind. The GP bundled Warren and his mum off to a paediatrician.

Diagnosis: autism. The cause? Who knows? The hallmarks? Three big ones:

- *these kids don't seek out or enjoy any sort of social interaction; the saddest thing of all is that they don't want to play*
- *their speech is late, slow and odd*
- *they get into narrow, stereotyped, ritualistic ways of behaving and developing interests.*

There was a lot of work to be done. Half of it was directed at Warren. The other half was directed at his family. The distress of these parents is enormous. Because just as most kids love to have hugs and cuddles, so do most parents want to give them. The pleasure of an embrace is that you get embraced back. It makes the arduous job of being a parent just that little more enjoyable.

Anthony was a cold fish. He was a house master at an exclusive private school. Good at his job. Intelligent. A competent disciplinarian. Dedicated and conscientious. But oh, so cold! The boys used to call him 'the Ice King'. Then one wit came back from school cadets with his new nickname: '2IC' (too icy).

Anthony appeared to have no desire for, or need of, close human contact. He was friendless but not lonely. Needless to say he was single and no one knew much about his family. He appeared to have little or no contact with them. Or anyone for that matter. Rumour had it that many years previously he had laughed at a joke. And never again since.

One of his contemporaries from his own school days bumped into him at a fete one day. He recalled how Anthony had been a fairly 'normal' kid, if a bit quiet. So what had happened to him to make him so aloof and indifferent to the praise or criticism of others? No one knows. Some people just develop this way.

Diagnosis: the Schizoid Personality Disorder. Nothing to do with the illness called 'schizophrenia', but as we shall see below, schizophrenics are pretty isolative too. A rare but odd disorder. Eccentric loners. They make good hermits.

Betty was single, spinsterish, with grey hair in a bun, no make-up (why bother?) and she lived alone. Always had done. She'll probably die alone too.

Not that she was cold. Far from it. A charming old woman. And she got on with all her neighbours because of her warmth and generosity. She was also very popular with her workmates down at the café. She was a cook there (she would never be so bold as to call herself a 'chef') and had been so for more years than anyone could remember. Constancy. That's what Betty liked.

She had lots of friends and doted on her many nieces and nephews. So what was missing from her life? Would I enrage my female readers if I said it? What was missing from her life was a man. Or a woman if that was her fancy. Just someone to have an intimate relationship with. Someone to have some head–stomach love with, you know, like a pair of old slippers. Someone to depend upon.

Had she ever had one? Even when she was a pretty young woman with lipstick on? The owner of the café had known her to go out with one man, a decade or three ago, but only for a couple of dates. Rumour had it that she'd had her heart broken by a bounder with a seductive smile and a woman in every café down the highway.

So that was Betty. Nice, but isolative. A highly functioning loner.

Diagnosis: an avoidant personality. Often found in people who have had their fingers burned in relationships. They decide that they'll give them a miss in future. They're fresh out of trust.

The avoidant personality. Not even a personality disorder, since she did not seem to be distressed by her aloneness and perhaps she got on better in life without some man hanging around cluttering it up. Or did she? And does anyone really want to live alone for the rest of their lives?

Cedric. Now he had a life story to tell. Quite a normal sort of young man. Then he went mad. Stark raving. They locked him up in a psychiatric hospital after he was found wandering the streets at night, dishevelled, half-dressed, talking to himself and shouting abuse at someone. But there was no one there . . .

Diagnosis: schizophrenia. The hallmarks of this condition are:

♦ delusions. He thought that the CIA were following him. But that wasn't so bad because God had given him some sacred stones to throw at them when they popped up.

♦ hallucinations. Voices in his head that tormented him. They mocked him and told him to kill himself and be done with it.

♦ 'thought disorder'. Jumbled up, chaotic thought processes.

♦ emotional lability. He was all over the place, from elation to depression to panic to anger. All in the space of two minutes.

♦ 'psychosocial deterioration'. He'd started his career at university, then dropped out, then got a job as a bank teller, then as a labourer, then went onto the dole, then went mad, then ended up on the pension. In the process his friends just sort of drifted away. Downhill all the way.

After he was discharged from hospital he spent many years living in a boarding house. Alone. A bit like Anthony, the cold fish. But there were two reasons that Cedric avoided people. The first was that relating to people required such an effort. He didn't enjoy it any more. So he gave up. The second reason was that he was so preoccupied with the world inside his own head *that he didn't seem to need any external stimulation. He just sat there thinking his strange thoughts and listening to his voices. All day. Every day.*

HOW TO DEAL WITH THE LONER

It depends upon what type of loner you're talking about. As you can see, loners come in different shapes and colours.

If you're talking about autistics and schizophrenics then be aware that there are all sorts of medical bodies and support groups who deal with these loners and their distressed families.

Schizoids are beyond anyone's reach. It's rare for them to seek help from anyone medical or paramedical. They just float through life with their moat around them and no desire to drop the drawbridge.

Now avoidant personalities are another thing. Within every avoidant personality there's a dependent one trying to get out. But usually it is quite inaccessible. It's the trust thing again. And the fear of abandonment. You have to be around an avoidant personality before they allow themselves to *believe* that they have a drawbridge. And usually they don't wait around that long. That's why they're called *avoidant* . . .

 # The Bloke

I am about to give fifty-one per cent of the world's population a little glimpse into the mindset of the other forty-nine per cent. Blokes. You think we're painful. We know we're pain-full. It's just that we can't own up to it. And lots of blokes can't even see it. Poor sods.

We blokes have been given a lot of bad press over the past decade or two. There is a group of the fifty-one per centers who believe that every man is responsible for every injustice ever perpetrated upon any woman. Look, I know that we're not squeaky clean but, please, *give us a break!*

Men and women are different. Not just between the legs. We are different in how we think. And what we have to endure in life.

CASE HISTORY

David ran into a problem from the moment of conception. He copped a Y chromosome. He was in big trouble.

When he was born his parents deliberated over whether they should mutilate his genitals. They thought that by slicing into some of his most important skin they would help him to be clean. Thankfully they decided against it. Phew! He spent the rest of his life washing under his foreskin whenever he had a shower. No big deal. Quite enjoyable in fact.

At puberty the problems in his life quadrupled. Now his hormones began to give him hell. Acne. Growth spurts. Wet dreams (he thought he had some disease) and learning how to masturbate. Then clumsy attempts at chatting up girls. And phoning them with sweaty palms because he was sure that they would tell him to go take a hike.

He needed his Dad around at this time. As a role model. To talk to about blokes' stuff. And to see how men were supposed to treat women. But his Dad was at work. And when he was home he was emotionally walled-in.

Then rugby. Barely controlled violence on a paddock. But at least some cameraderie. Funny how blokes feel united by mock warfare and a few beers afterwards.

All through his early adulthood was the need to compete and do well. Sports, work, women. But he was no oil painting to look at and pretty average in the IQ department. If he didn't strive and succeed then he was a nothing, a nobody. Life was getting harder.

After having his heart broken by a couple of women, he met and married Eleanor. A good woman. They produced a couple of brats and did the suburban thing. By this time the burden of responsibility was weighing on his shoulders. And his coronary arteries. If he didn't work and bring home the bacon then the family would lose everything. All these people relied upon him. He would sit at the end of the table since he was the 'head' of the household. But he didn't make too many of the big decisions. Lots of responsibility and only the illusion of power.

David also became familiar with the First Law of Marriage. It states that 'in a marriage, the person with less libido rules the sex life'. The person with more libido is the more needy. That's a position of weakness. The person with less libido becomes the 'gatekeeper' to their sexual activity. That's a position of strength. In most marriages it's men who have more libido. Or at least fast, hot libido. Women's libido is more like a steam-train: it takes a while to get going but then you can't stop it. So David found himself having to ask Eleanor for sex. He stayed faithful to her but in his fantasies he would find himself satisfying a super-model. Men have all the power, he would hear the feminists say. But when he was on his knees begging Eleanor for 'a bit' he didn't feel very powerful at all . . .

In his heart David knew what he felt. He felt lonely. His wife could chat so easily with her friends. She spent an hour a day on the phone just 'networking'. But when David had a night with the boys it centred around drinking too much and letting each other know how well they were doing. One-upping in other words.

Then came the mid-life crisis. Depression, futility, loneliness. No direction. No identity, no power, no meaning, no joy in living.

He sort of struggled through it and carried on. Always keeping his pain to himself. He hung on a few more years but his coronary arteries went into retirement before he did. He died early. Men usually do.

Sad, isn't it, how we men go through life. Psychologically there are three main characteristics that separate us from the other fifty-one per cent. You'd better own up to them because you've only got the rest of your short life to try to work on them.

They are:

- ♦ the Me-up mentality. We have to be the best. We can't stop competing. We judge our self-worth on our wealth, power, fame and status. If we have none we're worth nothing. We have no sense of *peace* in our lives.
- ♦ the Me-out mentality. We build emotional walls around ourselves. We hide our tears. We've been trained to do this from an early age. We were mocked for crying then. We don't let anyone get too close – in case they're gay. Or people think we are. We live in a state of unrelenting homophobia. When we communicate it's to pass on information. Men are into *report*-style communication while women are into *rapport*-style communication. That's why our telephone conversations last twenty seconds and theirs last twenty minutes.

♦ the 'left-brain' mentality. We think that the world is a logical place. That it can be understood using rationality. That logic is something to be followed from point A to point B to point C, etc. We believe that for every problem there is a solution. We reduce things to their simplest form. Ha ha. Get real. Women don't see things that way. They tolerate ambiguity. They are eternally patient. They don't need to pursue reason or solutions. They generate hypotheses, not deductions. It's called 'heuristic' thinking. Right-brain stuff. And we men are dead losses at it.

HOW TO DEAL WITH BLOKES

Start by giving us a break. Help us along. Let us admit to being little boys dressed up in business suits. Encourage us to weep. Don't snigger when you hear about those funny 'men's groups'. Take some of this responsibility off our backs and give us some true power, not just the stuff that we try to gain with our fists.

So that's all about blokes. Now we'll pause while I let my blood pressure come down and then we can turn the page and get on with the book . . .

The professional victim and the compulsive Rescuer

I have elected to describe these two Painful People together. There is a very simple reason. Like Tarzan and Jane, like yin and yang, like meat pies and tomato sauce, *they are always found together.* Most times they also form a triangle with a third character who is known as the Aggressor.

Let me also point out that the Professional Victim (PV) is usually a tad more painful than the Compulsive Rescuer (CR) who is slightly more pain-full. Either way you get the drift. There's a lot of pain floating around here.

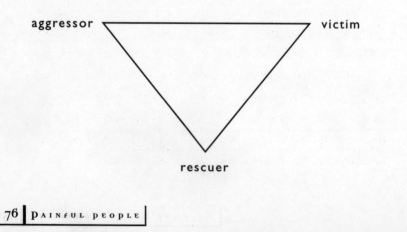

Frances was a professional victim. Now don't get me wrong. We're all victims from time to time. When our houses are burgled, or we get run over by a passing truck, we're victims. No two ways about it. But Frances was more than that. She was a professional.

Frances relied heavily upon our old favourite defence mechanism: projection. Whenever anything bad happened to Frances she could always find someone to blame. She had an unshakeable belief in her own goodness and rightness. And innocence.

The neighbour's dog was always barking. Their children were awfully rude too. The local council was incompetent and do you think that the government will do anything about it even though she's written to her local member? Of course not. And then there was her battle with the Pensions Review Board. How do they expect anyone to live on that pittance of a pension? If only Frances' daughter would help her but oh no. She was too selfishly caught up in her own life. And poor Frances here at home with her gammy leg and that bowel of hers. Oh, it caused her so much agony.

When Frances said words like 'agony' she could make the listener feel in pain. It was pronounced 'aaaagoonnyyy'. As she said it she would wrinkle her face up in a grimace. For effect.

We all know what happened to Frances' daughter. She got so heartily fed up with her mother's whingeing that she left home and never went back. She would phone her mother from time to time and then put the receiver down for ten minutes as her mother talked at her. About all her many problems.

Into this web, spun by the PV, wandered the CR. Her name was Joan. A mild-mannered compassionate woman. Joan believed that her works of charity would get her into heaven. After a few weeks of trying to rescue Frances she found that they had got her into hell.

Joan helped Frances write to the council again. Joan phoned Frances' daughter and dropped a guilt trip onto her. The daughter told her where to get off, then burst out laughing and hung up. Joan drove Frances around to her various doctors, her chiropractor, her homeopath and then down to the sea for a frolic in the waves. Skipping through the surf made Frances look surprisingly healthy.

What Joan, in her benign selfless naivety, didn't realise was that not even Mother Teresa could rescue Frances. Frances was a bottomless pit of need. The world would always do Frances wrong. Even if she won Lotto she would be miserable. She sort of, dare I say it, enjoyed her misery. But she eventually exhausted and alienated everyone else. Including the every-loving long-suffering Joan.

Finally Joan spat the dummy. She told Frances that she could no longer be at her beck and call. In a very softly spoken and charitable way, of course. But Joan had no idea how badly Frances would react to this. The wrath of a thousand dark angels fell upon Joan.

Frances came out fighting. With her acidic tongue she tore the hapless Joan to shreds. Joan stumbled away from this encounter feeling battered and bruised. She never went back. It took her a few months to recover from this. But then she got back to her rescuing work. A little older and wiser perhaps.

And Frances? She began to whinge to all and sundry about the incorrigible selfishness of that bitch Joan.

COMMENT

You've seen it played out hundreds of times. The PV broadcasts her problems on all frequencies. They are like a spider's web waiting for a fly called the 'CR' to become hopelessly entangled. The CR is a well-intentioned person with a 'do-goody' mentality who has difficulty with disappointing people. But why do some people have to be so holier-than-thou? CRs often have a number of personality characteristics in common. A bit of the Limpet. A fear of abandonment/disapproval/rejection. An overgrown sense of self-control and duty. A tendency to hunt in packs (the Volunteer's Brigade, St Someone-or-other's Legion, the committee that sends food parcels to the refugees in M'bongoland). Yes, I know that they do good work. Yes, I know that they help the underdog. But sometimes, just sometimes, the CR reveals a bit of their own dark side. Along with the beat-me-beat-me-masochism is a narcissistic sense of moral self-righteousness. A smugness that suggests that they have in their pockets a one-way ticket to heaven that you and I, poor sinners, are sadly lacking.

HOW TO DEAL WITH THE PV AND THE CR

The United Nations used to have a motto: give a man a fish and you'll feed him for a day; teach him how to fish and you'll feed him for his lifetime. The message so pristine in its simplicity. It says stop rescuing people and help them to be self-sufficient. Rescuing is like a M'bongoland food parcel. It has to be rationed. Love is like trust and forgiveness. It can never be unconditional.

And keep in mind, all you CRs, that in the PV's mind you are always dispensable. My years in psychiatry have taught me three very simple truisms:

1 An alcoholic will find a drink on a desert island.
2 A person who wants to commit suicide will do just that.
3 A Professional Victim *will always find a rescuer*.

The moral of the story is that we should all *rescue* amateur victims, like kids, refugees and the impoverished. But doing a 'caped crusader' routine on a *professional* victim is going to end up with your cape all tangled up in a sticky web.

 The failure

There are some people who just fail in life. They snatch defeat from the jaws of victory. Again and again and again. They shoot themselves in the foot so often that they seem to be walking around on stumps. I call them *the Failure* – for obvious reasons.

Now let's look at the converse. What do you have to do in life to be a Success? You have to cross plenty of life's hurdles.

EXERCISE

This is an exercise in being a Success. Or an Olympic hurdler.

❶ First, you have to cling onto life. Avoid famine, plague, bus crashes and psychotic stepfathers with claw hammers and a bad attitude.

❷ Now you have to get some education and training. So that you've got a ticket. So that at those cocktail parties with the liquor and the showing-off you can tell people that your name is . . . and you are a . . .

❸ Now you have to hold down a job, with all the endless hassles and Monday-morning frustrations involved in that. There's not a lot of kudos in being on the dole.

❹ Now you have to nurture a network of friends and maintain a decent sort of intimate relationship. And there are every-day-of-the-week frustrations in that.

❺ Now you have to do something a bit special. Win a prize. Show a bit of talent. Marry a millionaire. Do something heroic in a bank hold-up. Make sure you get your fifteen minutes of fame. And then see if you can stretch it to, say, an hour or two.

❻ Now you're a tall poppy and you have to make sure that the envious masses don't come at you with a pair of scissors.

See? It's not as easy as it looks.

THE WOT OF SUCCESS

So what are the characteristics that one needs in order to become successful? There are a number of groups on the Seminar Circuit who try to convince all the thousands of people who attend their courses that everyone can one day be ruler of the world. Easy. Just pay them a big fat cheque and then spend a weekend getting pumped up by a half-dozen Americans with the gift of the gab, some colour slides of mansions and Mercedes Benzes. Pardon me if my cynicism is showing. You see ninety-nine per cent of the suckers who attend these courses go home to their former obscurity and the other one per cent always had a filthy rich grand-daddy who was just about to fall off his perch.

The characteristics of successful people are summed up in the acronym WOT. That stands for Wisdom, Opportunity and Talent.

WOT = Wisdom + Opportunity + Talent

By *Wisdom* I refer to that elusive personality trait that is a combination of being street-smart, learning from your mistakes without being beaten down by them, reading the *process* beneath the *content*, knowing when to shut up, and being patient. That's why we usually associate wisdom with age.

By *Opportunity* I refer to the observation that you can have all the wisdom and talent in the world but if you're hanging out for a food parcel in M'bongoland it amounts to nothing. However, if your wealthy old grand-daddy starts complaining of chest pain you'd better pay him a lot of attention and chat to him about revising his will.

By *Talent* I refer to the observation that if you're going to be a successful accountant it helps to be good at numbers; if you're going to be the next La Stupenda it helps to be able to sing; if you're going to be a brain surgeon you might have to get rid of that tremor; and if you're going to be a barrister you'll have to dump the stutter.

So that's success. Enough already. Let's go back to failure. Be aware that there are three basic types of distress, like the three primary colours. They are anger, anxiety and sadness.

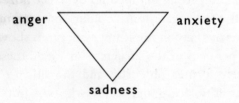

The three basic types of emotional distress

I lump together the concepts of sadness and depression for convenience's sake. Even though they're by no means synonymous. We'll put that one under the microscope in the section on 'Depression'. So hang onto your breathless anticipation.

Q: So what's all this to do with the Failure?

A: When I encounter people who habitually fail in life I try to work out whether they are mainly into passive-avoidance (anxiety), lack of drive (depression) or passive-aggression (anger). Confused? Good. Read on.

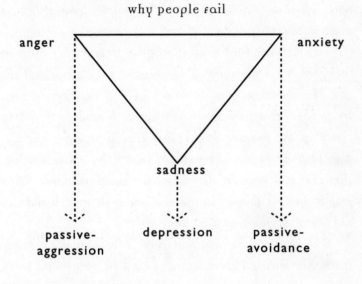

why people fail

CASE HISTORY

Brenda was a bank teller. Had been for about four decades. With forty years' experience under her belt she was a pretty good bank teller. When she felt those banknotes flick beneath her gnarled fingers and smelled the odour of a thousand people's pockets and wallets waft from them she felt at home. The clink of coins, the tap-tap of the calculator, the crisp flick of the rubber bands around yet another wad. Ah, bliss.

Her customers knew her well. Some of them had grown old with her. Other bank tellers in her branch had come and gone. They'd been young, just as she'd been on that terrifying first day when she had served her first customer. A ball of nerves. Now she could do it in her sleep. Sometimes in her dreams the odour, the clink, the tap-tap and the crisp flick visit her again. And in her nightmares she receives glowers from the manager, and redundancy notices. In four years' time she would have to retire. Those were the bank rules. The prospect terrified her. So much so that she put a lot of effort into not thinking about it.

So what happened to all those other tellers? They went on to bigger and better things. Management traineeships and the like. The obnoxious ones would get a bit of seniority and then try to boss her around. They had left her behind on their long climb up the banking ladder. But Brenda stayed where she was. Holding in her annoyance at those who did better than she did but politely declining the occasional offer of a promotion. 'No, thank you, I know how to do my job and I'm not interested in learning anything else.'

The strange thing was that Brenda was actually a bright spark. She knew all about orchids, which she grew on the small patio space of her apartment, where she lived alone. She could do the daily cryptic crossword in about fifteen minutes and was irritated if there was just one last stubborn word that refused to reveal itself. In the local art gallery she could explain the subtle differences between the various schools of art with a professorial confidence. Lots of talent. Not a lot of success.

Brenda's problem was passive-avoidance. The fearful evasion of taking any risk. The over-riding need to have security and constancy. She had grown up being exposed to unrelenting messages about the dangers of the world. Her tyrannical father would go on and on about communism, capitalism, consumerism and Catholicism. There were reds under every bed. Along with the pirates and polar bears. Bad vibes to be exposed to when you're just a little girl trying to learn who to trust.

To Brenda responsibility was a dirty word. It was for other people to have. They would be the managers and she would be the staff. They would be the government and she would be the voter. They would be the clergy and she would be the parishioner. They would be active and she would be passive. It was safer that way. This wasn't humility. It was fear. Of falling on her face; of failure; of rejection; of living life to the full.

CASE HISTORY

Craig was the manager at Brenda's bank. He had worked alongside Brenda when he was fresh out of school, full of enthusiasm, hormones and pimples. Craig's enthusiasm had caught the eye of the Powers That Be in the bank and he had been offered a traineeship. He thought that all his Christmases had come at once. He went at it like a bat out of banking hell. Long hours of tertiary education after work. A Bachelor of Banking, if such a thing existed, proudly hung on his office wall. His own office, not one to be shared with the minions. His name on the door. Conferences where he could rub shoulders with other bank managers. Something to call himself at those cocktail parties. Hello, my name's Craig and I'm a bank manager.

But just when Craig was becoming ripe for promotion from Smallsville to the Big City Branch, his enthusiasm ran out. He became quiet, introverted, broody, irritable. His smile faded and his work performance dropped off. He struggled to put on a brave face but his laughter sounded hollow. Like Queen Victoria, the Powers That Be were not amused. And so, for years on end, Craig was stuck in the misery of Smallsville. Struggling to think, concentrate or make decisions.

When he finally went off on sick leave, the staff were told that he had contracted a virus and would be bedridden for a few months. Then a rumour went around that an ambulance had been seen outside his house and they had taken him to that big brick psychiatric hospital on the outskirts of Smallsville because he'd taken an overdose of sleeping pills. In such a small town you can't keep down a wonderful, juicy piece of gossip like this. It spread like wildfire. The bank manager had gone bonkers.

Three months later Craig returned to work. Fragile, but fairly well recovered. He was loaded up to the gunnels with anti-depressants that gave him a dry mouth but also gave him some hope, confidence and dignity. He was back on track again, after years of quiet, suffocating depression. Unrecognised and undiagnosed until he couldn't go on. He had hung onto his misery. Why? Because he's a typical bloody bloke, that's why. Now he had his sights set on the Big City Branch and he was going to wow the Powers That Be or die trying.

Later that week the staff heard a strange noise coming from Craig's office. He was on the phone to someone. He was laughing. They hadn't heard him laugh for years.

CASE HISTORY
_____

David was a saboteur. Not one who would attach mines to Greenpeace ships or hack into the World Bank computer *system. David sabotaged himself. He only just managed to get into university and then continually failed his exams there. He would sweet-talk his way back the next year but as the exams loomed closer he found other things to do: watching TV, playing tennis, chatting on the phone, sleeping, lazing around. He knew what he was doing but found it almost impossible to make himself sit down with his books. As he dilly-dallied he was almost weeping with frustration. He was bright enough; all he had to do was a teensy bit of swat.*

Then he would fail his exams. Again.

Eventually the university threw him out so then he charmed his way into a job. He attended the job interview in his best suit. He spoke clearly and eloquently and enthusiasm oozed from every pore. But when he got the job he slipped back into his old ways again. Showing up late. Allowing himself to be easily distracted. Long lunches. Always seeming to be on some sort of one-man 'go-slow'. Throwing sickies. Failing to show up to meetings and appointments. It looked as if David didn't really want this job but was too lazy or too ignorant to resign. But herein lies the rub. David didn't want to fail. He knew that he was on that long course again. It was inevitable. He would shoot himself in the foot and then they would turf him out.

David was both frustrated and frustrating. He concealed a perfect fifty-fifty mix of the painful (frustrating) and the pain-full (frustrated). His modus operandi was to procrastinate, delay, under-perform, refuse to co-operate. And then somehow he would be punished. Usually by being given the shove.

Amongst all this free-floating frustration was an immense amount of anger. David had a big chip on his shoulder and whenever he encountered an authority figure he went automatically into sabotage mode. He knew what he was doing but he couldn't stop it. He lived in a quiet state of resentment, particularly if he felt that anyone had power over him. But early on in life he had discovered that he had a weapon of extraordinary force. It was sabotage. Passive-aggression. The ability to bring someone to their knees begging for just a little bit of co-operation. Before you drive us all crazy!

Karl Marx said that the only power a worker has is to withdraw his labour. When workers go on strike they show management just how much power they have and how they are to be respected. But there's a problem here. Passive-aggression is effective but inefficient. Yes, the workers could ruin a company and yes, David could disempower all his bosses. But the workers didn't get paid while they were on strike and David kept ending up on the dole queue. Passive-aggression is like a bomb that unleashes your murderous rage but blows you up in the process.

So why was David hell-bent upon being a short poppy? His father had been the ultimate authority figure. David, like all painful adolescents, was supposed to be the prince who dethroned the king. Fathers, on the other hand, are supposed to graciously surrender their power to the next generation so that their sons can feel like men. Throw in a few oddball incestuous themes and there you have it: the Oedipal struggle. David's father wasn't going to be dethroned by a funny-looking son whom he didn't even particularly like. So he crushed David's fledgling self-esteem as if it were a gnat. That's when David stumbled upon his secret weapon. His passive-aggression enraged his father. David was regularly exposed to bucketsful of abuse. But he derived a deep pleasure from seeing his father's face turn red and those ugly veins in his neck stick out. What a glorious weapon he had. But what a burden of frustration he would bear for the rest of his life . . .

The next time you're working in a team that is accomplishing little and carries on in a milieu of unrelenting frustration look for the David in your midst. He'll be the one with the taunting little smile.

HOW TO DEAL WITH THE FAILURE

Despite the obvious fatigue of your grey matter, remember the triangle of emotional distress. Try to work out whether the Failure is being fuelled by anxiety, sadness or anger. What you do depends upon what the fuel is.

- ♦ passive-avoidant people are often best left where they are. Every beehive has to have worker bees. We can't all be queens and drones. If a passive-avoidant person can summon the courage to address his or her insecurities then they need support and encouragement to be assertive, education in leadership techniques and continual reassurance that they are allowed to make mistakes.
- ♦ depressed people need to see a shrink. Don't let me sound elitist here but I also feel that they should see a psychiatrist rather than a psychologist. Despite our very appropriate dislike of taking pills there are times when getting some chemicals into your body is the fastest way out of the tormented hell that is depression. Let's not romanticise it.

Craig's years of depression were wasted years. Life's too short for that.

♦ passive–aggressive people are the hard ones. I have learned from bitter experience that if someone wants to sabotage then there is nothing in the world that anyone else can do to stop it. The more influencing or activating people become with saboteurs, the more passive and destructive the saboteurs become. The only people who can do anything for saboteurs are the saboteurs themselves. The more energetic and enthusiastic you become the more inert and stubborn they become. And then you notice the taunting little smile. Sometimes the only thing you can do for a passive-aggressive person is to walk away. This ends 'the game'. After all, what's the point of staying on strike if the factory has closed down and the company gone bust. A basic biological principle is that *the perfect parasite doesn't destroy its host.*

consider this

You're in the supermarket with your toddler, who is grumpy, tired and fractious. Toddler decides that he's going to sit down, right here in the supermarket, and refuse to budge until he is picked up, taken home and put to bed. Paediatric passive-aggression. You try to soothe him and cajole him into getting his chubby little backside off the supermarket floor so that you can get on with this loathsome task of shopping. You know somewhere in your heart that if you die right now you'll go straight to heaven. Even the martyrs didn't have to put up with this. Bad news. Toddler is staying put. A David in the making. So you take your supermarket trolley and walk away. Down the aisle and around the corner. The game is over. What does toddler do? He gets the aforementioned bum off the floor tiles and runs to find you. The rest of the trip to the supermarket is not wonderful but at least toddler keeps toddling.

# The borderline

Shakespeare said that 'hell hath no fury like a woman scorned'. He evidently hadn't met any borderlines. They have enough fury to start World War Three. And do it with the sweetest smile. They are like those spiders who mate and then devour the male. Seductive but deadly. Attractive but acidic.

Borderlines are nearly always women. They rank among the most painful of people. When men are unendingly painful they usually end up being narcissists or psychopaths. Women, on the other hand, end up as borderlines.

CASE HISTORY

Amanda was, you guessed it, a borderline. When you first encountered Amanda you were immediately impressed by her charm and warmth. Only later, when she had her claws into you did it dawn on you that Amanda, like all borderlines, had a sixth sense about everyone she met. Within seconds of talking to you for the first time she knew two things about you: how you could be flattered and how you could be hurt. She knew what made you feel good but she also knew what your Achilles heel was. A sophisticated borderline can do both of these with extraordinary force, yet with subtlety. The iron fist in the velvet glove. When you walked away from talking to Amanda you were left with powerfully good or powerfully bad feelings. The good feelings were related to the little seductive glow that she gave off. The bad feelings were related to the little barbs, intensely personal ones, that she had popped into the conversation, just to remind you that she knew your vulnerabilities.

Amanda had a history of intense, transient, unstable relationships. They followed the same pattern. Lots of heart–genital love as described in Paradigm 7. The old pattern: encounter, attraction, fantasy, seduction, idealisation, disappointment, disillusionment, rage, rejection and then start the whole cycle again. At cocktail parties she could show off with the best of them. And usually end up taking some infatuated guy home. Her relationships with both men and women were never boring but neither were they calm, stable or comfortable.

That should have made Amanda just about the most powerful women in the world. Not so. Her ability to manipulate was matched only by her sense of torment. When Amanda experienced too much stress she would fall apart like the frothing monsters that appeared in her nightmares. One of her boyfriends dumped her after she had decked him. Her rage had become uncontainable. Later in the pub he joked with his mates about how he had been thumped in the bottom of a rugby scrum. To admit that his glamorous girlfriend had floored him with one well-aimed punch to his left eye-socket was too much humiliation to bear. Battered boyfriends? No one at the pub had even heard of that notion. Of course they believed him and thought what a hard-case bloke he was.

Beneath Amanda's business suit and make-up was a tortured little girl who worked at a very primitive level. Denial, splitting and projection as described in Paradigm 6.

The sad little girl who lived inside Amanda had a dark secret: she was terrified of being alone. Abandonment and rejection. The very thought of them made her frantic. She didn't cling like a limpet. No, she was too clever to make it so obvious. From an early age she had learned the three weapons of manipulation: intimidation, seduction and guilt. That's how she controlled people. She hoped that she would get them to hang around. But then the rage appeared again and she repelled them like the wrong end of the magnet.

Emotionally Amanda was all over the place. When she was happy she was a little too happy. During those times she was the life and soul of the (cocktail) party. Attractive, vibrant, enthusiastic. But it wouldn't take much for her to drop into the pits of brooding despair. Just a little disappointment, a jest that would go wrong, the slightest insult, the most minor threat of rejection. Then whammo, the shrieking, threatening, eye-socket-punching shrew would return.

Now let me give you another glimpse into the tortured mind beneath the stylish coiffure. At times in her life Amanda would do the strangest things. Twice she went mad, but only for a day or two. It's called the 'micropsychosis'. A little trip into insanity. Her mistrust would become paranoid delusions. Her instability would become chaos. This is how borderlines got their name: because they always seem to be on the borderline *of madness.*

Twice she had taken overdoses, not necessarily to kill herself, but certainly to attract the attention that ensued. Borderlines sometimes do this. It's called the 'parasuicide'. At the time they convince themselves that they want to die, but they invariably take overdoses of relatively innocuous drugs and they often phone a 'rescuer' and announce what they have just done. Sometimes borderlines accidentally commit suicide. *This is probably what happened to the highly neurotic poet Sylvia Plath, who gassed herself in her own oven on a day when her husband or housekeeper was supposed to arrive home to 'rescue' her but was delayed for an hour or two.*

If you think that this is becoming more and more peculiar then cop this: on three occasions Amanda cut herself. Each episode of self-mutilation followed a similar course of events. It began with a sullen phase of brooding that was followed by an escalating and out-of-control feeling of non-specific emotional pain. During this spiral of distress Amanda would begin to get the psychotic feelings back again. Things did not seem real. She did not seem real. She seemed to be moving out of her own body, just as people who have near-death experiences report. But Amanda's sense of being dissociated from her body was accompanied by the most profound feelings of panic and horror. Amanda knew instinctively what she had to do. She would find something sharp. A razor-blade or a shard of glass from the window that she had just punched in. Then she would cut herself. Not to sever the arteries in her wrists and then bleed to death. No, she cut herself so that she could see her own blood. *She needed to do this in order to* feel real.

Such an idea is incomprehensible to anyone but a borderline and be aware that not all borderlines are self-mutilators and not all self-mutilators are borderlines.

If you could ever gain access to the inner mind of Amanda, if you could look into her soul, then you would find a little girl in pain. And an exquisite sense of emptiness and barrenness. Get the picture? We are dealing here with a very disturbed young woman. More acutely disturbed than the derelict schizophrenics that you see in bus shelters downtown. More disturbed than just about anyone. But all hidden behind a face that is sometimes charming and warm.

HOW TO DEAL WITH THE BORDERLINE

So how do you handle the Borderline? The answer is simple: Borderlines, like bubonic bacteria, are to be avoided. Some highly trained psychoanalytically oriented psychiatrists can help them but it requires a fair amount of commitment on the part of the Borderline, a whole lot of time (think in terms of years, not months) and a psychotherapist who has the patience of Job. When they come to see me professionally I find my nervous tic coming back and something in the pit of my stomach goes into spasm. Psychiatric warning bells. I admire my colleagues who can treat Borderlines. I have a very simple philosophy of life: there are two ways to live your life and they are the easy way and the hard way. Becoming involved with Borderlines, personally or professionally, is the hard way.

 The Hypochondriac

So here you are at the cocktail party. Everyone is dressed in their finery and those drunken skites are over in that corner. You get caught in a different part of the room talking to a little old lady who is listing her illnesses for you. She's *always* had a bad back and her bunions are giving her hell. You didn't particularly want to hear about her botched haemorrhoid operation but she's going to tell you anyway. She gets a headache every other day and from her description it becomes obvious that no one in the world could ever have a headache that is as severe as hers, not even Amanda's boyfriend. Or perhaps someone with a meat cleaver embedded in their forehead. As she goes on, and bloody on, you find yourself daydreaming about what she would look like with a meat cleaver right there. It would give her blue-rinsed hair a sort of surgical parting. You wish you were back with those inebriated show-offs. They might be well and truly up themselves but at least they aren't boring.

You have met plenty of these little old ladies before. You might be a truckdriver or a shop assistant but she's going to give you her medical history come hell or high water. She doesn't seem to notice that your eyes have glazed over and you're looking longingly over at the show-offs.

A psychoanalyst would be able to describe this behaviour away very succinctly. To be a patient is to assume a regressed, child-like role that is designed to elicit care. Most people go to see a doctor with some reluctance and look upon hospitals as places to avoid: they smell of disinfectant and in their basements there are refrigerators full of people who didn't make it out the front door. But some people just love to be a patient. Hospitalisation? No

interface between physical and emotional pain

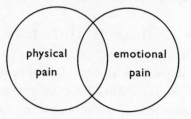

problem. Referral to a specialist? Can't wait. Investigations that involve a tube in every orifice? Where do I sign?

You see there is an interface between physical and emotional pain. In its simplest form it can be stated like this: if you are depressed then all of your physical pain becomes worse; on the other hand if you are in physical pain for long enough then you'll get depressed.

consider this

Your boss is Amanda. She's had a bad day and she's making damned sure that you'll have one too. You're frazzled, fazed and fractious. Last night you scored a bad case of *shagger's back* (you shouldn't show off so much in bed). It didn't bother you then but all of a sudden it's started to ache. Just as Amanda shares some of her mental pain with you, your physical pain gets worse. Surprise, surprise.

now consider this

Your back has been sore for years since you tried to save your little old grandmother some money by single-handedly shifting her grand piano from the basement to the second storey. Every time you try to show off in bed it gives you jip. And it's not just the pleasures of the flesh that are tricky. So are sitting in one position for too long or lifting anything heavier than a hamburger. You wish that you could have gorilla arms to use to tie up your shoelaces. From time to time you have to spend a mind-numbing week on 'bedrest' (which is medical terminology for domestic imprisonment) and after that you stagger around within a corset that would have done Queen Victoria proud. So what happens? After years of being a slave to the lumbar demon you get depressed. More surprises . . .

Ergo there is an interface between physical and emotional pain.

And now back to that awful old woman who had you bailed up at that never-ending cocktail party. You think that she's a hypochondriac, don't you? That's because you haven't been reading your psychiatric textbooks recently. The whingeing woman with the piles is actually a *somatiser*. She has a myriad of undiagnosed and undiagnosable problems. They become part of her personality. Somewhere inside she is hurting emotionally but she can't quite find or define that suffering. So she describes it somatically. With a hundred symptoms spoken to a hundred strangers. Anyone who would lend an ear.

So what's a hypochondriac?

C A S E   H I S T O R Y
_____

Christine was a beautician. You know, those pretty women who wear too much make-up and gossip all day. Christine was a dab hand at those plastic fingernails that look like talons. Her head was an encyclopaedia of the neighbourhood scandals. She was really good at her job. She could cake your face in mud, chew gum and give you the dirt on everyone's love affairs all at the same time. What a woman.

Over the last few months she had developed a nagging cough. In the cool of her sleepless nights she began to worry about this. It started as a concern that she might have lung cancer. Then it grew into an obsession. She convinced herself that she was riddled with fungating tumour. It would be only a matter of time before she would have to hand in her nailfile and go to the great salon in the sky.

So she trotted off to her GP, Dr Thomas, who was an ageing, obese chap with bushy eyebrows. The eyebrows raised a quarter of an inch when Christine told her story. Dr T slapped his stethoscope onto Christine's chest and then sent her off for blood tests and X-rays. There, he said, all clear. No cancer. Nothing to worry about. Go back to your facials and your blusher and think no more about it. Christine thanked him profusely and left his surgery breathing the city air into her pristine lungs.

End of story? Not likely. Christine was not like you and me, who can take the good news and get back to the cocktail party. No, she was a hypochondriac. You see, these are people who become convinced that they have an illness, usually cancer. But hypochondriacs these days are more and more seizing upon the possibility of their having an HIV infection. They have all the appropriate pathology tests and then go away reassured. For a time. But after a while the nagging doubts return. They obsess over and over. Did Dr T get it right? Should I have seen a specialist. After all, these medical tests aren't foolproof you know. We read in the newspaper every other day about some quack getting things tragically wrong. And that cough has been around for months now. Getting worse even.

So back goes Christine to see Dr T. His bushy eyebrows raise three quarters of an inch when she returns. He does the tests again. Still crystal clear. No crab-shaped masses gumming up her bronchi. Christine senses Dr T's surprise and feels silly. The next time the cancer-phobia hits her (which it inevitably does) she decides to seek another opinion: she presents herself to Dr Sarah around the corner. Dr S does everything that Dr T has done already. Many more X-rays and she'll be glowing in the dark.

There's the old pattern developing. A fear of a life-threatening illness and not a single soul in the world who can really, truly reassure the patient. Or at least not permanently. Now that's hypochondriasis. The real McCoy. Not so much a personality style as a lifestyle.

HOW TO DEAL WITH THE HYPCHONDRIAC

All you have to do is humour the Hypochondriac and then sweetly suggest that they talk it over with a professional. A mind doctor, not a cancer one. And don't panic, because if you do, they will too. Also, when it becomes obvious that their cancer-phobia is getting a little out of control *don't* laugh at them and *do* discourage them from getting their fourteenth and fifteenth opinion.

Hypochondriacs aren't horribly common but we've all come across one or two in our lives. They vary from the mild (who at least understand the cycle of reassurance and doubt) to the severe (who probably never have any true insight). The latter group are a wretched lot. A life of terror and doctor-shopping. And vulnerability to the con-jobs done by all the charlatans in the world who treat your cancer with vitamin C and apricot kernels.

The multiple personality

You've seen it on 'Oprah'. Now get the psychiatric angle on it.

❶ Go down to your local video store.

❷ Now ferret out the film *Sybil* from all the dusty old classics down the back. It stars Sally Fields but she's not so 'cutesy' in this role.

❸ Don't watch it if the Amandas of the world have given you a rough day or if you grew up in an orphanage and didn't have such a crash-hot childhood yourself. Also don't watch it late at night unless you don't have a lot to do the next morning. You'll be up all night with nightmares. You see, this is a heavy, heavy movie about an awfully abused young girl who grows up with a dozen-or-so different personalities. For most of the viewing audience this is just a horror movie with a bit of freaky psychiatric stuff thrown in. But there are people out there who actually do have 'multiple personalities'. Most of them have a history of childhood abuse (almost always sexual abuse is prominent) and life is not exactly a bowl of cherries for them.

❹ Now thank your lucky stars that you're just *you* and not *them*.

COMMENT

Just as you're getting a handle on the idea of Multiple Personality Disorder let me confuse you just a little more: the Americans have recently renamed it. They now call it 'Dissociative Identity Disorder'. Yes, I know it's all just terminology, but for once the Yanks got it right. Their term is much more accurate. This is not so much a personality disorder but something even more profound. It's not just about a habitual way of feeling, relating and acting. It's a major problem with *identity*. At the risk of sounding a little Buddhist here (the sound of one hand clapping and all that) identity is all about our concept of that thing that we refer to when we say 'I'. Now mull over that one.

Sufferers of MPD (or DID, whichever side of the Atlantic you bear allegiance to), rely heavily upon an old and reliable defence mechanism that is called *dissociation*. And what, I hear you ask in a unified voice, is *dissociation*?

Dissociation is the ability of the mind to split things up, cut things off, take parts of the mind and separate them so that they no longer associate. We dissociate in the face of nastiness or emotional pain. Dissociation can range from something that is common and benign to something like Sybil's condition. By now you'll be getting a headache trying to grasp this concept, so I'll give you some practical examples.

E X E R C I S E

❶ Go on a long bus trip. Not downtown, but over to that other city that's about ten hours' drive away. And no sleeping pills. That's cheating.

❷ You can spend only so much time reading, looking at the view and chatting to the old woman in the seat next to you about her illnesses. That takes up, say, an hour. The old woman in the next seat has fallen asleep and by her snoring it would seem that her lungs are working pretty well after all. Now you're faced with nine boring hours of bumping down the highway. So what do you do next?

❸ You daydream. You're on a bus in the middle of nowhere with a dangerous degree of understimulation. This is like being put into 'the cooler' in the prisoner-of-war camp. Not a lot of entertainment down there. Just like you and the snoring gremlin next door for the next nine hours. Your mind wanders. Grating memories of an argument you had. Flashes of rather pleasing erotic fantasy about that highly attractive person sitting across the aisle. Images of you telling your boss where to get off. A piece of music that you can't get out of your head. What a wonderful escape from the complete ordinariness of this bus trip. A healthy sort of dissociation. Your body is sitting here in the cooler but in your mind you're hanging off a chandelier somewhere.

CASE HISTORY

David was a chartered accountant. His profession has a bit of a public image problem but I can sympathise with that.

Behind David's business suit and button-down shirt was a heart full of pain. David's clients had no idea. He was the consummate professional. Calculators, dividends, receiverships, loopholes and banks that have run out of black ink. This was David's professional world. And his personal world? Full of memories of being raped at boarding school by one of the teachers. Behind the profit and loss and the numbers in brackets was a torment that ended up in a prescription for anti-depressants and weekly sessions.

It took David ten sessions to settle into the swing of his therapy. And about a hundred sessions to trust his therapist. Two years. Two full years of skirting around the issue. He alluded to the rape. He resisted his therapist's subtle pressure to return to the scene of that most horrible crime. But slowly he came around to it. It would be the next session, he decided. At last he needed to talk about it. To get it all out into the open in this 'safe' environment. To weep and cry out in rage and pain as he had been doing silently for all those years.

But he 'forgot' to come to his session. After religiously attending for all that time. He just 'forgot'.

Dissociation. It emerged from his horror of confronting his abuse. Anything to avoid the anger and humiliation again. His mind took the time of his next appointment and put it into the 'too hard' basket. He 'forgot'.

CASE HISTORY

Alpha company's trench on the battlefield stank of sweat, dysentery and fear. The balloon was going up. Private Jones knew what that meant. It was soldier jargon for time to go over the top and run towards the enemy machine guns. He had felt so proud when he signed up. A parade down the main street and pretty girls throwing flowers at him. His fantasy was to return heavily laden with medals and win the heart of Angela, his angel, who worked in the post office and flirted with him so much that he would find any excuse to mail anything to anywhere. And now here he was: surrounded by death and the distant sound of his old friend lying in no-man's-land and calling for his mother. Jones was stinking, dirty and trying to hold onto his bowels.

When the whistle blew he went into automatic mode. Up the ladder. Running towards some cracking noise in the smoke. Strangely calm. Waiting for the wet, red pain in his chest. The young soldier beside him went down with a bullet in the groin. Then Jonesy went down. No pain. He just couldn't run any more. He marvelled at how painless his death had been. As his face hit the dust he could see his name engraved on the war memorial in the main street just as his Uncle Charlie's had been. *And he could smell that musty post office counter. With just a hint of perfume.*

They carted him off to the Regimental Aid Post. He was surprised to be alive. When the smoke and clamour cleared he noticed that there was a crisp, clear blue sky. The doctor in khaki examined him. Jonesy knew that there must be a bullet hole somewhere near his spine. He couldn't walk. Or feel anything in his legs. But there was no bullet hole. Apart from the lice his pale skin was intact. It had been some self-protective part of Jonesy's mind that had made him fall down. Stupid man, it had said. Don't you know that you're running towards people who want to kill you? You must run no further. So down he went.

Dissociation. It can take a physical function and shut it down. Like speaking a painful truth. Or seeing a painful sight. Mutism and blindness suddenly appear. In these cases it's called a 'conversion reaction' but the process is the same: cutting off one part or function of the mind. For protection.

CASE HISTORY

Anne spent most of her life unemployed. She lived in boarding houses or government-sponsored accommodation. She had 'earned' this by several years of 'street kid' life. She preferred the roof over her head in the grotty boarding houses to the misery of life on the streets. In those days she would trade sex for money or food or accommodation. Once she lived with an abusive man who was an amateur truck driver and a professional thief. But he punched her and raped her once too often so she went back to sleeping in doorways. Even Anne drew the line at violence although it took her six months (and the return of summer) to pack her plastic bags and get out. Her emotional world, what was left of it, was characterised by fear, guilt, depression and deep bitterness.

Anne refused to be called 'Annie'. That's what she had been called when she was a little girl and was sexually abused in two of those foster homes that she had lived in. I won't go into all the gory details. This chapter is getting you depressed enough without another blow-by-blow. Now Annie was Anne and that little girl with pigtails and tears in her eyes was a million miles away. Most of the time.

In the drawers of one boarding house Anne had found, apparently amongst her own clothes, a leather skirt and frilly blouse. Sexy stuff. She initially presumed that the last resident had left it there. Then slowly it dawned on her. But how had they mysteriously moved overnight from the bottom drawer to the top drawer?

Veronica did it. Veronica was one of Anne's other identities. Anne sort of knew about Veronica. Sort of. She didn't worry about the sexy clothes. Some part of her knew that Veronica would wear them. When she went down to the pub and wowed all the men with her provocative jokes, her innuendoes and her wise-cracks to the barman. Then Veronica was confident, in control and seductive. A woman who could strut her stuff. Veronica could walk the walk and talk the talk. She stood in stark contrast to meek, masochistic Anne. While Anne was pain-full, Veronica could be painful.

But they were both the same person. And then Anne got a glimpse of another identity within her. It was a little girl. Anne did not know her name, just that she had pigtails and tears. Sometimes the little girl in Anne's mind would come to visit *and Anne would sit in her room hour after hour rocking backwards and forwards to comfort herself.*

Dissociative Identity Disorder. Them. *If daydreaming is a tiff, DID is global nuclear war.*

How to deal with the Multiple Personality

Don't. Send them to a shrink. *Post-haste.* And find a shrink who can deal with a patient who needs a lot of attention over a lot of time.

Also, keep in mind two things:

♦ lots of people who rely on these extreme forms of dissociation are simply too impaired to develop a constructive and trusting relationship with a therapist. And given the traumas that they've endured, can you blame them?

♦ don't entertain the fantasy that all the identities will one day fall into a huge psychotherapeutic blender and be spat out as one reconstructed person. Get real. The damage is usually too broad and too deep. Sometimes the only thing that can be done is an amelioration of the suffering. An empathic ear and (for the first time in their wretched lives) a constructive relationship.

The Restless

No, this is not a chapter about soap operas. If you think the case histories here will be about characters called 'Spike' or 'Randy' then think again. This is about people who are habitually restless.

Sometimes even exceptionally, endlessly, inexorably restless. Restless with a capital R. Now you've got the picture.

First let me deal with the childhood disorder that is called Attention Deficit Disorder. As always, just as we get used to a term like this the Americans go and change it. They now call it 'Attention Deficit Hyperactivity Disorder'. Does that seem a little pedantic to you? Yeah, me too . . . So to avoid giving you another headache I'll refer to it by the old acronym: ADD.

CASE HISTORY

Jack appeared to be a handsome little seven-year-old kid. He had a ready smile and was full of energy. That was the problem. Jack had so much energy it was oozing through his pores. Like most kids with ADD his problems fell into two main areas: inattention *and* hyperactivity.

At school he would spend more time gazing out the window at the birds and clouds than watching the blackboard. He could be enthralled by something that interested him. For about two seconds. Then he would be twitching and fidgeting, waiting for the next few moments of interest. To organise things, to listen to instructions, to set his fickle mind to even the simplest task, these were anathema to Jack. He went through school uniforms like a hayfever sufferer goes through paper tissues. Why? Because he kept losing them. And homework? He would manage a few lines of scribble and then be into monstering one of his brothers. Or waking the baby.

'Sit still.' Jack had heard those words so often that his flighty mind had learned how to 'unhear' them. He would shake and squirm in his seat. At the dinner table he would get half-way through his meal before he would be up and flicking

through the TV channels. It got so bad that the remote control was declared 'off limits' to our Jack but he was at it again a minute later.

Jack's mother slowly sank into despair. She loved him dearly but if we all have a cross to bear in life, hers was Jack and he was getting too heavy. At night she dreamed of him chained to a chair with his mouth being taped. She managed to struggle on because of her two daily 'oases': when Jack went to school (he could wear his teachers out then) and when he was asleep. Jack's father adopted the male response: he hid behind the newspaper and tried not to notice what was happening around him. The family strain caused all sorts of problems. To use a quaint Californian term, the family sort of became dysfunctional.

Sure, all kids are pretty active. And plenty of mothers drag their perfectly normal youngsters along to the doctor with the complaint that 'he must have this ADD thing that I've read about'. But Jack was more than active. He was hyperactive. *Over-the-top active. Every-waking-minute active. Not-a-bloody-moment's-rest active.*

So that's ADD. Rather paradoxically it may be caused by a problem in the brain that does not allow enough stimulation in. That's why some doctors treat this condition quite successfully with amphetamines which are, of course, not sedatives but *stimulants*. Kids with ADD are like visually impaired people who need bright light to see things, or partially deaf people who need clear sounds to hear. So it is with ADD kids: they need lots of stimulation to penetrate their bored brains.

And another thing. There is a trend these days to diagnose ADD in adults. Once again the Americans do this more than anyone else. But then again they also like to 'medicalise' plenty of things that the rest of the world considers to be part of the Human Condition. In the 1960s fat kids in the USA were dragged off to see doctors in the hope that there was 'something wrong with his glands'. The expectation is that there is a diagnosis and a pill to fix everything. After all, that's what doctors are for, isn't it? Think again. And nowadays there is the mysterious condition called Chronic Fatigue Syndrome, which is undoubtedly a real illness in some people but which has rather contemptuously been called 'yuppie flu' by those who think that it's just *acopia* (the inability to cope).

I have no doubt that some kids with ADD don't outgrow their condition, although most seem to. But be aware that before you diagnose yourself and trot off to get some prescribed 'speed', not every restless adult is hanging onto a remnant of previously undiagnosed childhood ADD. There is a group of adults whom we often encounter who appear to be very restless. They are driven people, often highly successful, but they pay for their drive. They seem to have no peace of mind. Within them you can sense an atmosphere that can be at best energising and at worst persecutory. There is no single word in English that describes this atmosphere. That's why I call it the *ERB* feeling. That stands for *Empty-Restless-Bored*.

ERB = Empty + Restless + Bored

Now don't get me wrong. We all have a bit of ERB. To have *a bit* of it is actually a good thing. It gives us our drive. It never lets us get complacent. Our ERB reminds us that it's all very well to be *here* (in this place, lifestyle, career, technology, belief system, whatever) but it looks a lot better over *there*. It promotes striving, ambition, change. When Robert Kennedy gave the speech at his brother's funeral he uttered the famous words: . . . 'some men see what is and say "why?" My brother saw what could be and said "why not?" . . .'

That's ERB. It's a hunger. To the psychoanalyst it is a hunger for mother's love. A hunger to feel comfortable, content, secure. Also to have meaning. When people have got their acts together they find that their ERB is quite manageable. But when it becomes severe, the ERB feeling can be tormenting. Take it to the wrong end of the scale and it can be associated with feeling hollow or 'like a shell'. It doesn't take much to tip that pain even further, when it is experienced as a fragmentation, a shattering, an annihilation. The Borderline and the Narcissist generally have far too much ERB. So do the Lost, whom you'll encounter a few pages down the road. If all this sounds a little queer to you then you can sit back and feel smug. You are doing a sterling job by keeping your ERB in check. If you identify with feelings of hollowness or fragmentation then you're in for a rough trot in life.

CASE HISTORY

Jack was a successful businessman. He cut a trim figure in his blue suit with his standard-issue red tie even if it made him look a bit like a flag. And he wasn't shy about pounding the boardroom table. He was driven. To earn, to achieve, to accomplish. He never finished a cup of tea because there was always a report to be read and a fax to be sent. His wife and kids saw him briefly, late at night, when he came home, threw a few words in their direction and headed for the study. He loved them. Sort of. But he loved the cut and thrust of business even more.

To reward him for being a competent captain of this ship of industry he regularly took home a bit fat pay cheque which helped him to buy his waterfront mansion in Richburgh. He was the envy of his underlings (who looked much more flaggish than he did) and was dined out by politicians seeking 'donations'. Talk about important.

Then the inevitable happened. In a corporate coup his company was 'taken over' (which is business-speak for the modern equivalent of rape, pillage and plunder) and Jack was forced into retirement. His blue suits were inhabited by moths and the mansion began to look a little frayed around the edges. So he sold up and moved from Richburgh to Middleburgh. Trouble was, Jack was as restless as all hell. He'd always moaned about the levels of stress that he'd endured during his celebrity career but now he lived every day drowning in needling, frustrating ERB. In fact it was not until he had his first heart attack that he began to slow down. He came to realise that he had to find peace somehow or his ERB would accompany him to his grave. So he took up fishing. Long meditative hours casting a fly into a stream. And he learned how to hug his wife again. And talk to her. Just like in the old days.

Twelve years later when he died in a hospice in Lowburgh he seemed happy to close his eyes and search for the final peace.

C A S E   H I S T O R Y
_____

Helen was a Borderline. Like Amanda. She knew all about ERB since she was plagued by it in her every waking hour. She felt empty all the time. Over the years she had found ways of 'filling herself up', so to speak, although none of them lasted for long. First there was food, which she would take in bulimic*

_____

* Rest easy. Not all Borderlines are bulimic and not all bulimics are Borderline. Phew, I hear you say . . .

binges that would make her feel full while she was gorging herself and then fill her with remorse and self-disgust as she vomited it all back up again. Then there were drugs. She really felt alive when she was grooving on Ecstasy or Speed. But she languished in the depths of misery the next day when the 'downer' descended upon her. Later there was sex. Lots of it. With men she met in bars and took to seedy motels. The seedier the better. Condom, shmondon. She liked to feel slutty. Somewhere in the back of her mind was an image of the man next door doing something to her when she was kid, but she tried not to think too much about it.

In the height of a sexfest she would even manage to score two men at once. Just for the hell of it. But as with the Ecstasy, she hated waking up the next morning.

What frantic efforts she went to in order to feel filled up, or 'real'. But they would last for only a few hours before her ERB returned to haunt her. So she lived her life like that: frantically. Looking for that elusive stimulation that would fill her up. Sex and drugs and rock and roll. And ERB.

CASE HISTORY

I'll tell you the saga of Jeff just so that you can keep in mind that ERB in little doses is not such a bad thing. You see, Jeff didn't have enough ERB. Or perhaps he had it and didn't know what to do with it. So he came across as being, well, lazy. He seemed to have no ambition. He settled for a low-paying job despite the fact that he was too talented and too bright to stay there. It wasn't because he had a big problem with self-esteem or was anxious and avoidant. He just couldn't see the *point of busting his gut climbing the ladder of life. He faced life as Jack did after his first heart attack. Something that should be struggle-free. Trouble was that he ended up in a rut in Lowburgh, bewildered at his lack of material comfort but not seeming to know the rules of the game of life.*

How to deal with your own ERB

❶ Quit your job. You never liked it anyway. Sell the farm. Do a runner. Get out of the rut.★

❷ Go and sit in a cave on a hillside somewhere. Alone. Study your navel for hours on end. Dine on locusts. Talk to no one. Read a lot of philosophical books that you can't understand.

❸ Do this for, say, a year. Notice that you slide into this hermit stuff a lot more easily after the first two weeks. That's why two-week holidays are nothing more than a teaser. Just as you're finally starting to wind down you have to go back to work again. So stretch this one out another fifty weeks or so.

❹ Now come down from the mountain. Beg for your job back. Buy another farm.

❺ Every ten years, go back to step (1) and repeat the exercise. That way you don't have to have a heart attack in order to learn how to relax.

★ Don't take me too literally here. I'm just trying to portray a scenario. So don't come whingeing to me if your bank manager hates you and your kids feel like orphans . . .

 **The**

psychopath

Psychopaths are the most Painful People of all. And the most damaged. The word means 'sick mind'. Read on and you'll understand why.

Every other night on TV you can see handsome, black-clad (but slightly nauseating) American policemen shoot one of these nasty people. Hollywood churns out dramas by the dozen that centre around some hapless psychopath copping a torsoful of lead in the final scene. Then you can switch off your television and go to bed content in the knowledge that the police really are well-groomed, muscle-bound avenging angels with God, and Smith and Wesson, on their side.

If only it were true.

But most psychopaths are not really acne-scarred weaklings with poor personal hygiene. Most psychopaths don't become involved in a string of fiendishly planned murders, each time leaving behind yet another clue to their identities. Most psychopaths do *not* set out to steal a nuclear weapon and hold the Western world to ransom. On the contrary, most psychopaths break in through your back door to pinch your video. And most psychopaths don't feel a compulsion to return to the scene of the crime. Unless, that is, they want to come back to get your jewellery. Indeed, most psychopaths are just awful ratbags who are as straight as a corkscrew and couldn't give a brass razoo (whatever that is) about anyone other than themselves. That's the essence of the psychopath: they are offensive, outrageous, obnoxious people who do whatever they bloody-well feel like. They have no regard for the rights of others and, worst of all, they don't seem to feel guilty about it.

Funny thing, this guilt. If you have too much of it you paralyse yourself. You can't put your own needs before those of others when you need to, so you end up stuck in the *give-love-care-rescue* routine until a Major Depression descends upon you and you end up seeing a shrink. On the other hand, if you don't have enough guilt then you end up seeing a lawyer.

I'll describe two types of psychopaths below. But first, a word about terminology. These days psychopaths are referred to with the term 'Antisocial Personality Disorder'. Or, alternatively, the 'Sociopath'. But all these labels refer to the same concept. People who transgress the rights of others. Like Eddie.

C A S E   H I S T O R Y

Eddie. You could feel sorry for him if it wasn't for the fact that he's just flogged your video off down at the pub to another psychopath to whom he gave the message 'if it don't work, just don't try to get it repaired or the cops'll be there when you go to pick it up'. The beauty of serial numbers.

The roots of Eddie's psychopathy lie in his past. Most other personality disorders become evident from adolescence onwards. But not psychopaths. Even as kids they're a pain in the bum.

His parents liked to blame 'the crowd he got in with' but that was just an example of projection that they used to comfort themselves. Eddie was a bully. He seemed to be involved in every schoolyard scrap. He pinched things whenever he thought that he could get away with it and when it came to shoplifting he was an artiste.

When the school toilet block burned down no one could pin it on Eddie. But they all knew that he did it. At the age of twelve he stole a car with some of his mates in 'the wrong crowd'. They went for a joyride and then took it to a nearby quarry, poured petrol over it and torched it. As some poor sucker's automotive pride and joy went up in flames Eddie felt the nice warm feeling that had been missing from his emotional world all his life. So the next weekend he torched a truck. For more warmth.

Four arrests later he found himself in a boys' home. This began his life of crime which was punctuated by frequent stays behind bars. Theft, assault, even a rape. He became very good at lying because of his admiration for the con-men that he met 'inside'. From them he learned that there is no point in telling little lies. People have more chance of believing big lies than little ones. He never assumed the identity of an ordinary bloke. No, Eddie would tell people, with a wink and a nod, that he was working undercover for 'a military intelligence organisation that I cannot name'. He knew who the gullible people were and he could fleece them good and proper. *He seemed to live for the moment, never planning more than the next con or heist. The day after tomorrow was too far away. He was impulsive, sometimes violent, always avoiding the police and the bailiffs. He could turn on a fatal charm and was good at picking up women in bars for a one-night stand, especially if he had nowhere else to sleep that night. He had three or four kids around the traps from three or four different women. But he never stayed around to watch them being born, let alone grow up.*

If he had he would have seen his progeny in the children's courts, just as he had been a generation before. Like father like son. Or daughter.

But the scariest thing about Eddie was the lack of guilt. Not a twinge. Unless it was turned on. An act to elicit sympathy and a bed for the night. And then he'd leave at four in the morning with his host's video recorder in his bag . . .

The Psychopath. Nasty, self-serving, violent, provocative people. Mostly men, but don't forget that there are women's jails too. A significant proportion of every prison population.

But not just blue collar level. Let me introduce you to Herbert. A white collar psychopath. In psychiatric terminology he might even attract the diagnosis of the *creative psychopath*.

C A S E   H I S T O R Y

Herbert was called Herbert because he wasn't allowed to be called Herbie. Such familiarity in Richburgh was considered vulgar. Herbert's daddy was a magnate. That means he was filthy rich. It also meant that Herbert hardly ever saw Daddy. Pater was gallivanting between the financial markets of New York and Paris and having dinner with arms dealers. So Herbert got dumped into an exclusive private boarding school. To Herbert that was like Eddie's boys' home. He grew up with other unloved, damaged kids who treated him brutally and made him brutal.

Herbert looked absolutely spiffing in a dark blue business suit with a red tie. You never would've picked him as a psychopath. But in business he was as violent with his power as Eddie had been with his fists. He would pick the prettiest secretaries and then coerce every one of them into having sex with him or losing her job. He had two mistresses whom he pampered with cars and apartments and then forced into sadomasochistic antics with him. And guess who was on top? Herbert, of course.

While Eddie was down at the pub quaffing beer, Herbert was on the forty-fourth storey doing cocaine. He had used some of his millions to import a suitcase full of it and his shady associates would distribute it around Richburgh. On the fifth trip his courier was 'busted' by customs. Herbert made sure that there would never be a shred of evidence against him. He had two middle-men executed by his hit-man so that they couldn't 'squeal' and then let the courier rot in prison for the next twenty years. And did he feel guilty? No, he didn't. Not even the teensiest bit. His only concern was how to find two more middle men and another courier . . .

Herbert could do a good con job as well. He was extremely charming. When he was on form (usually with a nostril full of white powder) he was the life and soul of the Saint Moritz set. But always looking to the Main Chance and who he could rip off. No bar-room brawls for Herbert. No lengthy jail terms (after all, he had minions to do that for him). Herbert didn't have to rob people taking a few dollars out of an automatic teller machine. He had offshore bank accounts and tricky-dicky accountants who could make millions disappear by pressing a button on a computer keyboard. While Eddie was washing his socks Herbert was laundering money . . .

The creative psychopath. Just a trumped-up Eddie.

First, learn a healthy degree of mistrust. If you find that you're being parted from your money then make sure that you're not a fool. Beware of charming liars whom you want to believe but you have this niggling discomfort about them somewhere deep in your grey matter.

Every society has a system for dealing with psychopaths. It's composed of a lot of police, courts and jails. It's inefficient as all hell but it's the best we human beings can do. No wonder the police get so 'burned out'. Wouldn't you if you met a dozen new Eddies every day?

And if you meet a charming man at a cocktail party who tries to convince you that he has 'the inside information' on a wonderful new investment that he will, reluctantly, let you in on as long as you throw a hundred grand his way, then I suggest you slip away and go back to the group of drunken boasters in the corner . . .

 **T h e   L i a r**

You thought that we'd covered this in an earlier section, right? The one about the Psychopath. So why stick in another section about people who lie? Because it's important to be able to know about the four types of lies, that's why. Yes, there are *four types of lies*. By 'lies' I refer to untruths, misinformation, the stuff you cannot or must not believe. In increasing order of intensity they are:

♦ white lies
♦ CRAP

♦ black lies

♦ delusions.

At the risk of sounding contrary, I'll start from the bottom and work up. Delusions. They're not really lies since the person telling them is convinced that they're true. The essence of a delusion is that it's an unshakeable, false belief and the person who voices the delusion is totally unaware that what they're saying sounds sort of screwy.

consider this

You haven't seen your neighbour's teenage son Richard for a few months. You bump into him at a local bus stop one day. He seems a little distracted and somehow different. His clothes are dishevelled and his hair needs a good wash. He's wearing a khaki-coloured overcoat with stains on it. His eyes have changed. Or at least the look in them has. They've lost their spark. He looks haggard and drawn and his eyes are wide and glance about furtively. You try to strike up a conversation while you're waiting for the Number 23 bus to come. It's heavy going at first. Then Richard begins to mumble away to you. It's all quite uncharacteristic. You begin to wonder whether he's been drinking too much or taking drugs. There's a whiff of stale something about him but you can't tell whether it's tobacco, beer or body odour. Or the lingering remains of marijuana.

Richard tells you that he has a gift from God. From his pocket he pulls out a grey-coloured stone which he holds in the palm of his hand for you to admire. It's like the millions of similar stones that anyone can pick up from the side of road in your area. He tells you that God has given it to him. It is his mission in life to free all caged animals and he will use the stone to unlock the cages at the zoo. And also the bird cages and rabbit hutches from every suburban home. The stone will release them all.

By this time you're getting fidgety. You have no doubt that Richard is in cuckoo-land and you're trying to remind yourself of the recent TV advertisements that pointed out that schizophrenics are mild-mannered people with an illness and not axe-wielding murderers. Nevertheless you're hoping that the blasted Number 23 bus would get a move on. As he is launching into a mumbled tirade about the agents from the CIA, the good old '23' comes around the corner. You get onto the bus. Richard stays standing where he was. He sees two men sitting in the back seats and looks fearfully away, raising his khaki overcoat collar so as not to be recognised. You cannot escape the impression that Richard thinks that these two men, who are engaged in light-hearted conversation, are CIA agents. So Richard will wait for the next '23' in the hope that it will be CIA-free.

The next day you see a photograph in the newspaper of a young man being arrested at the local zoo. It's Richard. He's still wearing the khaki overcoat with the collar pulled up around his ears. The newspaper reports that he had a rabbit in one of his overcoat's deep pockets and a grey stone in the other.

Richard was psychotic. No prizes for guessing that. What you heard were delusions. Richard was absolutely sure that they were right. God *had* given him the stone. His mission *was* to release all caged animals. Admirable. But very mad.

NOW consider this

There's a knock at your door. When you open it you find a short, stout man with a scar on his face. While Richard smelled unwashed, this man just smells nasty. You don't know it, but it's Eddie, the psychopath. You've never met him before and if you're lucky you'll never meet him again. But Eddie knows you. Or at least of you. You see, it was Eddie who stole your VCR last year and now he's come back to pinch the nice one that you just bought to replace it. What a nerve.

'Is Robert home?' says Eddie.

'No one called Robert lives here,' you reply.

Eddie's nasty little face breaks into an apologetic smile. He makes some noises about having the wrong house or the wrong road or something. Then he shuffles off. You watch him go. You have a bad feeling about this. Your hunch is right. Eddie was going to break in through your back door again, but he wanted to be sure that no one was home. He knows now that breaking into your house would not be so clever because you might object to his wandering out with your pristine new VCR. And you're bigger than he is. Eddie might be a ratbag but he's not stupid. He'll come back next Tuesday when he knows you'll be at work. Time to buy a Dobermann.

This was what I call a 'black lie'. Eddie knows damned well that no one called Robert lived at your house. He was just 'casing the joint'.

Also, be aware that there are some people who can tell volumes of lies, interlaced in a complex web of deception, and do this with a straight face. They inevitably harbour a fairly severe personality disorder. The phenomenon is called *pseudologia fantastica*. That's Latin for 'a whole pile of bullsh★★' . . .

So these are delusions and black lies. Now what's CRAP? It stands for *Confident Rationalisation And Projection*. It's not so much an exercise in lying as an exercise in denial and brain-washing. CRAP stops just short of being delusional. It's what the Narcissist, the Borderline, the Restless and a few other twisted souls tend to do. It's a wonderfully self-protective piece of mental gymnastics by which a person can twist things around in their own heads and come up with some version of the truth that suits them. And they really truly seem to believe it. So much so that they can sprout their CRAP with a convincing sort of confidence. And if you're a gullible soul and around a producer of CRAP for long enough then you'll come to believe it too. It's what the leaders of cults are good at. And they prey on poor souls who have a gap in their belief systems. A gap that's just itching to be filled up with CRAP.

The 'P' of CRAP is all about the fact that CRAP-artists rely so heavily on projection. That's the immutable belief in their own goodness, rightness and holiness. While everyone else is bad, wrong and sinful.

CASE HISTORY

John was the Big End of the Spanner and Joanne was his Little End. That means that he was an insufferable bully and she was his doormat. If you find a really good CRAP-artist, they're usually male.

Whatever went wrong in their lives was, in some way, blamed on Joanne. John could criticise her and put her down in the most awful ways. He did it with such supreme confidence that she began to believe it. Furthermore whenever she tried to go to him to thrash out some grievance with him he always managed to think quickly, talk quickly and do it with such confidence that he could turn her head around. She would begin the conversation in an angry mode, ready to point out to him how wrong he was and it would end up with her feeling guilty and ashamed for having been so ungrateful. Every time. Without even realising it John had discovered some of the techniques of mind control.

Little Ends usually go through a three-phase process: they get depressed, then they get angry, then they get out. That's what Joanne did. It took her about six months to recover from living with John's CRAP. Then one day she woke up and realised that she wasn't so bad, wrong and sinful after all. It wasn't until she could get away from John that she could establish her boundaries again and stop being an extension of John's identity. Like fleeing the cult.

So that's CRAP. And now the most common lie of all. The white lie.

consider this

You're at home and the phone rings. It's a Member Of The Opposite Sex. You recall meeting this MOTOS at a party the weekend before. He/she was a nerd, as you recall. Boring. And rather plain. The prospect of being wooed and cuddled by this MOTOS does not stir your hormones in the least. Tough luck. This MOTOS is asking you out. You think quickly. You're about to tell him/her that you already had something arranged for that night. No good. He/she will just ask you out some other time. Tell him/her you're gay? Not likely. Word will spread and all the other MOTOSs will stay away in droves. Washing your hair? Too corny, even if it would give him/her the message. So you tell him/her that you're in a relationship with another MOTOS even though you know that you've spent plenty of Saturday nights at home with the cat recently. In reality you yearn to be asked out by a MOTOS, but not this one.

The MOTOS sounds a little hurt but understanding.

You hang up with a sigh of relief. A guilty sigh, but a sigh of relief nevertheless. You have just told a white lie. It's called white because you feel guilty about it, but it's told so that you can cushion your feelings and the feelings of the other person. Most of the time we human beings are not as stupid as we look. We know when we're being told a white lie. We usually want to believe them. So we do. We don't want to be told that we're ugly geeks with absolutely no personality. We know that already. We want to be let down gently. There is something rather consoling about this white lie.

How to deal with the Liar

It all depends on what sort of lie you're being faced with. So the first step is to decide whether the lie is white, black, delusional or just CRAP.

For white lies, just grin and bear it. You tell white lies. I tell white lies. Where there is life there are white lies. They are mistruths that are designed to avoid hurt. Not so bad really. So put up and shut up.

For black lies, keep a high index of suspicion. We human beings spend most of our time trying to find the right amount of *trust* in those around us. Too much and you're paranoid. Too little and you're a sucker. When you come across black lies the answer is simple: don't believe the lies and be very wary of the liar.

If you live with someone who relies upon CRAP, you're in big trouble. When you're around them they're always right and you're always wrong. That can get you down if you hear it for years on end. You come to believe that you're wrong. Remember the three Cs? Cope, change or cut'n'run. You choose. Put up with it (and accept the destructive consequences), try to change it (by repeatedly refuting the projection) or get out of it. I know what I'd do. I'd pack my bags.

For delusions, call a psychiatrist. You can't argue against delusions. You can't convince anyone to give up their delusions. You can't trick people out of their delusions. You just have to medicate them.

 # The actress

I know, I know. I'm not supposed to use this word. Actresses and waitresses are like public loos: they've all gone unisex. These days you're an actor or a waiter no matter what gender you are. So died the comedienne, who's now a comedian. Etc., etc. But I'm going to hang onto the word Actress here because I'm going to discuss the type of personality that is described as being 'histrionic' or 'hysterical'. And they're mostly women. Hence the archaic term.

And while we're on these etymological matters, students of Greek will recognise where the words come from. *Hysteros* is Greek for uterus. Hence 'hysterectomy'. The Greeks decided that hysterical people were mostly women and women possessed an organ called the *hysteros*. So they put two and two together and worked out that hysteria must come from the womb. A smart formulation that would be admirable if it weren't so wrong. *Histrios* is Greek for 'the actor'. They tell a *history*, or story. Histrionic people truly are actors. Or, more accurately, actresses. The essential features of the histrionic personality is that they're so damned emotional and they use this emotionality as an attention-seeking strategy.

This is in keeping with the observation that when men are backed into a corner, when their defences are being worn down and they are fighting for their life or dignity *they become more controlling*. They become angry, aggressive, domineering and generally up themselves. This is called the 'narcissistic defence'. Or else they just become withdrawn, shut down and uncommunicative. Me-up or Me-out but never Me-down.

When women are in a similar corner they *become more care-eliciting*. This is called the 'histrionic defence'. It might not be politically correct to point that out and, yes, it might be a gross generalisation, but it rings true. The histrionic personality (i.e. the Actress) acts as if she lives her life in this corner. There is an air of emotional desperation about her. Fragile, dramatic women, actresses.

CASE HISTORY

Linda was great at cocktail parties but you could have too much of her. If the party and the punch were becoming a little flat, then Linda could stir things along. If she were in good form, that is. It would be a matter of hiding the lampshades until Linda left. She would be the centre of attention and call everyone 'Daaaarling'. She would wear her heart on her sleeve. When things were going well for her (i.e. not too much depression and an attentive audience) she could be seductive and entertaining. But if you caught her with a bad case of PMT then she would become provocative and nasty. That's what made being around Linda so hard. You never knew whether she was going to flatter you or devour you.

At the end of the party Linda looked as if she was waiting for the bouquet of flowers to be delivered to her on stage so that she could take a bow and wallow in the standing ovation. If she felt she was being ignored then she would make damned sure that she would be noticed. The theatre seemed to be in her blood but she was actually the third daughter of a grocer and a seamstress who seemed to be so busy just making ends meet that they didn't have much time for any of their kids. So Linda worked out how to get attention. And then she never stopped trying to get attention for the rest of her sad, dramatic life.

Trouble was, being around Linda was tiring. She could be flirtatious at times but at other times just downright provocative. She spent a lot of time preening. She had a wonderful sense of style but always went just a bit over the top with her clothes. Sometimes she just looked garish. As much as she was dramatic and the centre of attention she was also shallow. The sense of pathos that surrounded her was epitomised by her tendency to view acquaintances as her 'dearest friends'. That's because she had few friends and none of them was particularly 'dear'.

Linda went through a number of boyfriends until she met Frank. They complemented each other. She was erratic and dramatic. He was patient and saintly. He could be the Little End of her Spanner, she thought. Of course they got married. She needed him to stabilise her. There was no way that Linda could have married an overly emotional man. They would have been at each other's throats in an endless battle for the attention and admiration of others. And Frank could never have married a staid and sensible woman. His life had been too boring for him to marry a boring woman and live a life of unremitting boredom in a boring little suburb. No, he had to marry a Linda. She drove him crazy with her antics. But she added colour to his life.

Which leads me to the observation about couples. You see, when couples get together, there are some things that they just have to have in common. Like a similar level of intelligence. And a similar sense of humour. Some shared experience and a shared culture also help. But there are some things that they just have to have that are dissimilar. Like their emotionality. An emotional person is attracted to an unemotional person and vice versa. If two very emotional people get together they will either destroy each other or live the rest of their lives acting out the final scenes of a tense drama. Forever. If two very unemotional people get together they will never make true emotional contact. No intimacy. Together but not *together*. In the same marriage and bedroom, but not truly intimate. That's why the Lindas and Franks of this world seek each other out. Yin and yang. The canoe and her outrigger.

How to deal with the Actress

Lesson one: unless you're a Frank, don't marry her. You'll spend the rest of your brief, tempestuous marriage feeling as if you're sitting in the front stalls of an endlessly unfolding play. When you need to be loved and nurtured you'll come to the numbing realisation that she's so self-preoccupied that she can't really empathise with anyone other than herself. And her habit of flirting with other men (how else did she get you hooked?) will drive you insane with jealousy.

The Actress needs to be contained. That means she must be given the message that there are other people in the world who need care and attention. She won't like that. In fact that's an understatement. She'll spit tacks. Or fire. But if she is consistently shown that she can't cry 'wolf' twenty times a day and she can't use every social interaction as her stage then one day she'll mellow. But it might take twenty years and half-a-dozen Franks to show her. And keep in mind that the less she feels noticed the more histrionic she'll become.

One final thought. There are some jobs that just suit certain personality styles. Narcissists make good dictators. Psychopaths make good bank robbers. Schizoids make good astronauts, provided they don't have to share the cockpit with anyone else. And the Actress makes a good ... you guessed it ... actress. If you're a Frank then encourage your Linda to do some auditions. She could be worth millions ...

The obsessional

Obsessional types are the anal personalities. Not that they're circular and have body odour, but because they have such wonderful control of their anal sphincters. Confused? Read on.

The Obsessional is a sticky person. He (because they are usually a 'he' and not a 'she') is a perfectionist. His personality is characterised by his rigidity, his stubbornness, his meanness, his orderliness and his conscientiousness. He's a stickler for the rules. He's a hoarder because he can't stand throwing anything out for fear of one day finding that he needed it. So his office is full of dusty paper and his garage is full of junk. The obsessional loses the 'big picture' and becomes lost in the 'little picture'.

He's crippled by his workaholism but it's not because he wants wealth and promotion, it's because he feels safe within the confines and structure of the work environment. More so than at home, which is messy and chaotic and requires emotional input. Emotions, yuk! The Obsessional loves thoughts. Nice, crisp, clean thoughts. Not mucky, ill-defined, uncivilised emotions. If the Actress is day then the Obsessional is night.

Most of all, the Obsessional is *inflexible*. Because there is a need in life to work out what's important and what's not. The unimportant stuff, like junk in a garage, can be discarded in the name of progress, efficiency and compromise. That's 'big picture' stuff. But not to the Obsessional.

So what, I hear you ask, has all this got to do with bottoms? Once again, the name Sigmund Freud, patron saint of psychoanalysts, crops up. Freud thought that we all pass through a number of distinct stages of development. One of these occurs in early childhood when kids learn to poo in the right place, i.e. not in their nappies. (Adults whose parents were aficionados of Dr Spock will have been involved with all that potty-training nonsense. This made parents feel more powerful and children feel confused and intimidated.)

At the risk of sounding indelicate (or like British toilet humour) faeces can have a lot of emotional significance. They can be a source of pride such as when a toddler learns to poo in the potty and then show his admiring parents what a clever wee defaecator he is. They can also be a manifestation of terror since bowels tend to empty when people are faced with overwhelming threat. Hence the expression 'to sh** yourself'. Faeces can also become a weapon. My neighbour gets enraged since he thinks my dog does doo-doos on his lawn. I can't convince him that it's that awful mongrel up the road who's doing it. My neighbour gives me hateful looks while the mongrel chuckles behind his paw. When kids do this it's called *encopresis*. Another polite term is 'soiling'. That's when kids who should have been potty trained go around doing it in their pants. Unlike bedwetting, encopresis is *always* a sign of serious distress in the kid. An indication of thwarted rage or a cry for help. As you can see, a poo is a many-splendoured thing. And often highly emotional. That's why the Obsessional, to whom emotions are anathema, has a tight anal sphincter. The so-called Anal Personality.

Another thing. People can become obsessional as a defence mechanism. When people are overwhelmed with information or work, they can become excessively organised as a coping strategy. The problem is that they can become so obsessional that they don't achieve much. Once again, they begin to lose the 'big picture'. They are so busy tending to the trees that they lose sight of the forest. Also, old people who begin to dement (i.e. lose their memory, cognitive functions, etc.) often become obsessional. They make lists to help their memories and become regimented at home about where they store things because they know that their environment has to become extremely organised so that they will know where the hammer and the envelopes are even though they have no idea of what day it is today.

In layman's language, 'obsessionality' can cover a multitude of sins. I have separated out three styles of obsessionality, all of which overlap:

❶ the tendency to 'obsess', i.e. get stuck on a theme and be able to think of little else. Human beings habitually obsess over a predictable variety of topics.

❷ the obsessional personality, i.e. rigid people with tight sphincters.

❸ obsessive-compulsive disorder. You read about this a lot in women's magazines these days. This is a definable mental disorder in which people experience either obsession or compulsions or both. Check out the case histories below.

CASE HISTORY

Peter was besotted with his classmate Annette. They were both fourteen, both wore braces and both studied French together. He could think of nothing other than her plaits and the way he shivered when she said 'Je t'aime' to him behind the gym last week. He obsessed over her.

Theme number one: obsessional love. When adults do it they tend to get themselves into all sorts of sticky situations involving bedrooms and private investigators.

CASE HISTORY

Annette knew that Peter was besotted with her. She felt the same way. She loved every pimply inch of him. Even his braces were cute. Love is blind. Thank God for that. But when Annette looked at herself in the mirror all she could see was her gawkiness. Her plaits were just awful and her horrible metallic style made her laugh with her lips closed. Her girlish hips had become broad and womanly and she searched her adolescent magazines to find the right diet to slim them down without losing a millimetre off her smaller than average bustline. She tried to avoid looking in the mirror because she disgusted herself. In three years' time her father would make an off-hand comment about her weight that would trigger her into obsessional dieting and months of hospitalisation for anorexia.

Theme number two: obsessional self-recrimination.

CASE HISTORY

Philip lived next door to the Joneses. When they bought a luxury car he had to go deep into debt to buy a better one. When they put in a swimming pool he had the bulldozers in his backyard in the blink of an eye. When old man Jones joined Rotary, so did Phil. He become obsessed with keeping up with the Joneses.

But the thing that Phil simply couldn't stand was seeing Mrs Phil chatting to old man Jones across the fence. Was she having an affair with him? Who else had she chatted up like this?

Theme number three: obsessional jealousy.

CASE HISTORY

Captain Ahab stood on the windswept deck. Where was that accursed white whale now? He would hunt the beast through the seven seas. He would kill it and bathe in its blood. Or he would die trying. Which he did.

Theme number four: the obsessional desire for revenge.

CASE HISTORY

Paul was so obsessional that he became a Trappist monk. That meant that he could live his life in solitude, silence and severity. Obeying the rules. Never talking to another person. Never having his life cluttered by those mushy, dangerous things called 'intimacy' and 'sex'. But during all those years praying in his cell or chanting in the chapel he was plagued by a memory. It was the memory of succumbing to the temptations of the flesh with a straw-haired girl named Sarah when he was eighteen. He had grown up in the same town as she had, gone to school with her, been obsessed by her, flirted with her, kissed her, touched her, dreamed about her. Then one day the opportunity, her beauty and their hormones all fell together. Paul fled from this passion to the safety of the cloisters. But he obsessed over the girl with straw hair. And the guilt that he felt day after day after day.

Theme number five: obsessional guilt and self-recrimination. An inability to forgive oneself.

Andrew had a tight sphincter. He didn't just obsess about love, jealousy, guilt, etc. He was obsessional. As described above. Rigid, inflexible, sticky. A view of the trees and no concept of the forest.

Andrew worked as a postmaster in a small rural post office. Needless to say, this appealed to him. Routines, places to put the dockets, precisely kept opening hours, crisp brown envelopes, pay and allowances as per award, procedures spelt out in the post office manual. Ah, bliss.

Then one day the post office modernised. Gone was the old logo and in its place something despicable conjured up by those city advertising people with long, greasy hair and nostrils full of drugs. Pristine envelopes replaced with multi-coloured post-packs. Yuk! Cosy spotlighting to replace the fluorescent tube. A paint job so that his sanctuary was no longer grey, like the drizzling clouds of winter, but all pastelly and bright. It offended his eye. His beautiful, leather-bound, well-worn policy and procedures manual was to be replaced . . . by a computer disk!

The day the technology arrived, Andrew retired. It was all too much. Too much and too quickly. His haven would never be the same. So he spent his retirement living alone (as he always had) in his cottage with its grey walls and fluorescent lighting. He still got up at the same time every day but spent his time in a lonely limbo of retirement and when he died none of his neighbours knew of the years of depression that he had experienced while maintaining his garden and his routine and his grey walls so immaculately.

*If only he'd learned how to loosen up. How to see the Big
Picture. How to enjoy life rather than organise it. How to relax
his sphincter.*

CASE HISTORY

*Phillipa thought she was going mad. At least she knew that
she'd lost control of her mind. She had had an upset at work.
Just a minor tiff with her supervisor. But then she became
anxious and insecure. And then she started getting* the
thoughts.

*Thoughts? What thoughts? Recurring, intrusive, unwanted
thoughts with distressing themes. Violence, destruction, murder.
They would come slamming into her head with such force that
she would gasp. She had images of throwing her beloved three-
year-old son down the stairs. It was an image that appeared in
her head again and again. And when she was driving her car
down the street she felt the overwhelming urge to steer into the
path of an oncoming car. She would shudder and hold the
steering wheel with white knuckles until it passed.*

*Then after that settled down she went through a phase
of checking.*

*Checking? Checking what? Checking every bloody thing.
Whether doors were locked, whether every electrical appliance
was switched off before she left the house. She would check
everything in a set order and then repeat the ritual five times.
So it took her twenty-five minutes just to leave the house.
Then she would have to come back and go through it all once
or twice more, just to be sure. If she didn't, her head would be
filled with images of returning to find her own home burned to*

*the ground. So she would worry and tremble and sweat until
she came back, for just one more check.*

*Obsessive-compulsive disorder. Not quite the same thing
as obsessional love, jealousy, guilt, etc. And not necessarily
occurring in an obsessional personality. Obsessions are
thoughts; compulsions are actions. Obsessional thoughts have
a recurring number of themes such as dirt, disease,
contamination, violence, sex, blasphemy. Compulsions
become routines of behaviour that simply must be carried out
if the sufferer is to get through the day. Checking, counting,
washing, touching. Strange stuff. But common. And often
interpreted by the sufferer as being some sort of insanity.*

HOW TO DEAL WITH THE OBSESSIONAL

We all have something that we're obsessional about. Like eighteenth
century clocks, cricket scores, V8s or Peruvian history. No big deal.
We can even harbour obsessional love, jealousy, guilt, etc. For the
most part, these are just a part of the rich fabric of life. So don't
sweat about them. You don't necessarily need to be locked up.

Obsessive-compulsive disorder, on the other hand, is not a
madness but it can almost drive you mad. The good news is that
if you can get off your bum and go and seek treatment for it
there are some very effective techniques that can get the thoughts
and actions under control. The approach is called *cognitive-
behavioural* (i.e. *thinking-doing*) and sometimes some medications
help. Nothing that will zombify you and, after all, what do you
have to lose but a lot of nasty thoughts and some pretty peculiar
behaviour.

The obsessional personality is a rather harder nut to crack.
Obsessives have to be encouraged, over a period of time and in
a supportive environment, to chill out. They have to get the

message that even if the routines are not exactly adhered to then the world will not fall apart. Either that or they have to be given jobs as rural postmasters and left to live their anal existences as they please.

 ## The paranoid

First let me get a few things straight. I'm talking here about the paranoid personality, not the paranoid psychosis. So what's the difference?

consider this

You're a hippy. Problem is, you should've grown up and moved on some time in the 1970s but you stayed stuck in that phase. You call everybody 'man' and you wear kaftans and bandannas. Personal hygiene is not your *forte*. Macrobiotic vegetables are. The only aspect of hippiedom that you've (reluctantly) given up has been 'free love'. You had to because your partner got an enormous case of the sulks when you screwed around last summer so you've decided that monogamy might be boring but it saves a lot of drama at home.

You've just smoked the biggest joint that God ever created. Good old God. Giving us this wonderful weed. You're supposed to be floating off into a numbed state of introspective pleasure. But wait. Something's going wrong. You're getting edgy and twitchy. You begin to think that the other people in the room are laughing at you. Despite the fact that they're wearing their regulation kaftans you come to realise that they're actually undercover drug squad detectives. The cars driving down the street outside seem to be driving slowly today, as if pausing to photograph your house. The phone rings and your bowels turn to water. This must be the signal from the drug squad for the kaftan-wearing associates to spring the handguns and badges. But no, it's your Aunt Mabel asking you over for dinner on Sunday. Your friends go on rolling joints. You decide that you'd better give this stuff up or you'll end up on the funny farm.

See? A transient drug-induced psychosis. Now let's look at the real thing.

One day Terry went mad. Or at least he started to. The process began slowly and then gathered momentum. In the end he was stark raving.

Terry was a shop assistant. He sold TVs and VCRs in a big department store. He showed up in shirt and tie, neatly groomed, every working day and went home each evening with a feeling of a job well done. But one day he came to realise that he was being followed. When he walked down High Street there was always someone behind him. A different person each day. Once he stopped and looked back. He saw someone pause and look into a shop window. Him, thought Terry. It must be him. The next evening it was a her and then two more hims on the next two evenings. Soon he came to realise that there must be a they and he began to become preoccupied with them.

On one occasion he got home to realise that they had been there. He just knew. They must have steamed open his mail and moved a few things around. Nothing was missing. Oh, no, they were too clever to do that. They had broken in and gone through his things but tried to make it look as if everything was okay.

The next development was the clicking on the telephone and the hang-ups on his answering machine. They were tapping it. They had his number. When he changed it to a silent number they still somehow managed to get it. They must have friends in high places. He felt tormented. Why wouldn't they just leave him alone?

His friends noticed the change. Terry could no longer have 'happy hour' at the pub on a Friday evening because he kept saying that his beer tasted odd. Could it be poisoned? His friends tried to convince him that there would be no earthly reason for anyone to want to kill him. But this didn't dissuade Terry. He knew who it was. It was them. He didn't know why, but he just knew that they were persecuting him. And for some reason they wanted him dead.

It all came to a head one day when he rushed into the administration offices at work to tell them that there was a bomb planted in one of the VCRs in his department of the store. He knew. He had seen a man fiddling with the appliance and now it was ticking. The management weren't going to risk their good looks checking out the claim. They had no option. They cleared the store and called in the bomb squad. They interviewed Terry and everyone else on the scene. A sophisticated robot was sent in to remove the VCR and drag it into the carpark. Terry watched from afar with his fingers in his ears.

Of course there was no bomb. Half-way through the operation Terry told the police about them. They called in a doctor. The VCR ended up back on the shelf and Terry ended up in hospital. Knowing now that the police, the doctors, the department store staff . . . they were all them.

Paranoid psychosis. A type of madness. Lots of delusions. Fixed, false, persecutory ideas.

Now on to the Paranoid. A personality style. Trust is a two-phase process. The acute phase and the chronic phase. In the acute phase of trust we work on our gut feelings. We sense somewhere in the pit of our stomachs whether or not we can trust someone we've just met. Car salesmen want us to develop that with them instantly. Doctors and lawyers try to engender trust in them from the first meeting. But true trust is a more chronic thing. It is earned over a period of time by continual demonstrations of trustworthiness. That's why you shouldn't have screwed around last summer. Your partner will now take a long, long time to develop a trust in you. Perhaps he or she never will.

CASE HISTORY

Tom had a big problem with trust. He had an inherent belief in the nastiness, the malevolence of people. If you said something provocative in jest he would take it as the deepest insult. If you looked at him in any but the most benign way he interpreted it as a sneer. If you complimented him he would misconstrue it as an insult.

At work no one knew much about Tom's private life. He kept his cards close to his chest. He believed that if people knew too much about you then it gave them 'ammunition'. Tom was also famous for his ability to bear a grudge. One day one of his workmates, John, made a complaint about how cantankerous and fragile he was. In fact John's unofficial words were that Tom was 'an obnoxious pain in the bum'. Tom never forgot this slight. John learned the hard way that Tom could bear a grudge for decades. Eventually the two had to be separated and Tom went to a different department. But his new workmates rapidly discovered that within Tom lurked a tormented soul. Always on edge. Always oppressed. Touchy, oversensitive, stiff, defensive. Above all distrusting.

Tom lived with his overweight wife Jane. They had two overweight kids who had now grown up and left home. The kids had discovered, much to their relief, that the world wasn't such a hostile place overall. Perhaps Dad had been wrong. Perhaps most people are mostly good most of the time . . .

Tom's paranoid tendencies seemed to spill over at home. Despite the fact that Jane wasn't exactly an apparition of loveliness he became touchy if she ever spoke to another man. He would frequently accuse her in private of being unfaithful to him. She could talk him out of it. Sort of. But he never quite lost these jealous preoccupations. So Jane gave up talking to other men. Just to keep the paranoid peace.

John had been right. Tom was an obnoxious pain in the bum. Most paranoid personalities are. There is something that is permanently outraged about them. But beneath this anger there is a feeling of something more sinister and more pathetic: terror.

HOW TO DEAL WITH THE PARANOID

First the paranoid psychosis. The answer here is quite straightforward. Call in the men in white coats with the strait-jackets and the butterfly nets and get the Paranoid treated by a professional with some pretty heavy pills. Even then the prognosis for paranoid psychosis is not exactly rosy. If someone has a deeply entrenched paranoid delusional system then even the strongest anti-psychotic medication will often not budge it. But at least they can come to learn to live with their delusions. They can get on with life even if they always *do* know that *they* are around.

As for the paranoid personality, the best way to handle them is to avoid stressing them; do everything out in the open so that they can't accuse you of covert words or behaviour. Don't try to make them your friends and, above all, don't marry them. You'll end up in a cult.

And if you're an employer make damned sure that they never become the union rep.

 T h e   z e a l o t

Zealots are a mix of the Obsessional and the Paranoid. Every society has them. Their main characteristic is their fervour. They live their lives for their cause. Unfortunately this leads to a number of problems. They lose their own identity. They believe that they have the answer to the world's ills in one political/religious system. They lose all their old friends and family and hang around exclusively with other zealots who share their cause. They become evangelical. They skip and dance at their meetings to show that they are high on their cause. Their cause becomes the centre of their otherwise dull lives. They fill up the cavity of emptiness within themselves by embracing the cause. They're a boring lot.

❶ Pick a cult, any cult.

❷ Now join it.★

❸ Now give it all your time, attention, love and money. Most importantly of all, give it your every last penny. In a few years' time, if you ever shake yourself free from this cult it'll be the fact that you're stony broke that'll hurt most of all.

❹ Tell everyone about your cause. *Ad nauseam.* Take no notice of the eyes that are rolled or the doors slammed in your face.

❺ Now choose from the following methods of ending your life for the cause:

♦ crucifixion
♦ flinging yourself and your family from a fortress wall
♦ self-starvation in prison
♦ suicide bombing
♦ going down in a burning Spitfire
♦ poisoned cherry-flavoured cordial.

Go for something that involves a splat. You'll get your name in the history books.

❻ As your body disintegrates and you hear your mother weeping allow yourself to wonder whether this was all worth it.

Excuse me if my cynicism is showing. I think that zealots are the bane of humanity. I work on the principle that if you think the whole world is wrong and you're right then you'd better make

---

★ I don't really mean you to do this. It's just for dramatic effect. So don't come whingeing to me if you've just given all your loot away to some guru with no hair and lots of Rolls Royces.

sure you're not going potty. Can anything good come out of zealotry? Occasionally benefits appear. Like democracy and Christian charity. Some zealots initiate worthwhile change in society but most are just nutcases. And whatever happens it tends to involve bloodshed.

So how does one become a zealot? It's a four-phase process:

❶ the phase of emptiness, lost direction and brooding
❷ the conversion experience
❸ the evangelical phase
❹ the end phase: death, martyrdom or loss of faith.

Most of us spend part of our life in phase one. We all need a sense of direction. You'll read more about this when I describe the Lost. When you're in phase one you're a sucker to be converted. And that often happens with a bang.

CASE HISTORY
_____

Saul was riding down the road to Damascus. He'd heard that there were these bothersome people called 'Christians' there, so he was going to get rid of them. Not just shoo them out of town. He was going to show them the business end of a sword. Life in olden-days Syria was not exactly jumping but beheading a few Christians always brightened up an otherwise dreary Thursday afternoon.

Then bang! He was hit by lightning. Funny thing to come out of a crystal clear blue Syrian sky but there you have it. Or at least Saul had it. Right on the cranium.

By the time Saul had picked himself up and dusted himself off he had come to a number of rather unnerving realisations. He was blind. The first letter of his name had changed to 'P' and he had been a closet Christian all along.

Time to come out of the closet and miraculously get his sight back. Then on to lots of fervent Christian work and lots of evangelical writing.

The conversion experience is just like being hit by lightning. Sometimes people go into ecstatic religious states and see visions, bleeding icons and the sun dancing in the sky. It's like suddenly and dramatically being smitten with love. And just as psychotic. (Oops, there's my cynicism showing again . . .)

HOW TO DEAL WITH THE ZEALOT

I won't go on too much about this type of Painful Person. We all know them. Most of the time they mellow. All fervour has a use-by date. The worst zealots are those that go from cause to cause. We see people in the business world doing this when they get fads for this or that style of management. Fashion and entertainment are infiltrated by their own forms of the Zealot too. If they don't have the fervour they are overwhelmed by their own ERB. But I suppose that filling the emptiness with fervour is more constructive then filling it with sex and drugs. Unless it involves splatting bodies and weeping mothers.

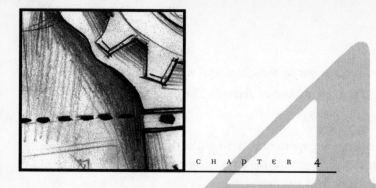

CHAPTER 4

SO WHAT'S A PREDICAMENT?

Good work. You've struggled bravely through the first two parts of *Painful People* and now you're on the final lap. Predicaments. You've had Paradigms and Personalities. Now for Predicaments. So what, I hear you ask, is a *Predicament*?

Predicaments are things that we can *all* encounter. Not many of us will be a Psychopath or a Hypochondriac or an Actress. For the most part Personalities are things that we begin to show in late adolescence and that we're then stuck with until wooden-box-time. But Predicaments are different. They're experiences that can be thrust upon us all. They are losses, mental illness, life events, developmental stages and painful roles. They can hit us today or tomorrow. They can come and go. Worst of all, *they can affect any of us*. So if you didn't identify with any of the Personalities described (and let's face it, you're kidding yourself if you didn't) then fasten your seatbelt. You're going to find your experience for sure in the Predicaments. Guaranteed.

So if you thought that Painful People referred to *them* and not *you* then close the book and go back to the protective cocoon of your own denial. We're all Painful or Pain-full People at some stage of our lives. So for the rest of you brave souls, read on and let's take a long look at the misadventures of life.

The
Depressed

So let's not muck around. Straight to the hard stuff, that's what I say. Here's a section about depression. Nasty stuff. So don't say I didn't warn you.

First, let's get a few definitions straight. When I talk about depression, I'm talking about an illness, not a mood. Not sadness or grief. They're covered in the section on the Grief-stricken. I'm talking here about a definable mental disorder with characteristic signs and symptoms that you'll find listed below. And don't think that it only applies to *them*: keep in mind that the latest research shows that about twenty per cent of the population experiences a clinical depression at some time in their lives. And I think that's a gross *underestimation*.

Okay, okay so I'm biased. I'm a psychiatrist. Surgeons come to believe that the whole world is scarred. Paediatricians come to believe that the whole world is 120 centimetres tall. Obstetricians come to believe that the whole world is pregnant. And psychiatrists come to believe that the whole world is depressed. But I'll stick by my gloomy observation. Depression, really bad depression, often masked by smiles and the appearances of normality, is as common as hell. Trust me.

Also let me remark how many people I encounter who don't know the meaning of the word. They think it refers to tough economic times or some lines on a weather map. Lucky them. So let me point out to you the two essential features of depression: sadness and *anhedonia*. Sadness is sadness. A down, flat, gloomy feeling. Tearfulness, which everyone experiences at times, but only women will admit to. And *anhedonia*? That's a difficulty in experiencing pleasure. Enjoying things. Getting a kick out of them. Just as a *hedonist* is someone who lives for pleasure, *anhedonia* is the absence thereof. Men find it easier to admit to this. Tears are not part of their vocabulary, but pleasure is.

Along with these two essential features are a whole list of others. Read on.

CASE HISTORY

One day Anne woke up and couldn't stop crying. She knew that this was coming. She knew that she'd been feeling wretched. She'd experienced it before. Many times. Once while she was at university, so that finishing her degree had taken five years. Once more before she got married. Because she knew that she should never have agreed to marry him and she felt trapped in a giant snowball careering down a hillside towards the final crunch that was her wedding day. Once more after the birth of her daughter; a post-natal depression that occurs after ten per cent of deliveries. Scary statistic, that. And now, her fourth, at the tender age of twenty-nine. Looking down the barrel of leaving her pain-in-the-neck husband. The prospect of being a solo mother. The prospect of divorce courts and loneliness and financial hardship.

She felt utterly immobilised. She resigned from her job. She retreated to her bed, drew the curtains and wanted to hide away from the world forever. She lived in a state of misery, agitation and dread. She couldn't sleep. She couldn't even think sometimes. She felt fogged up in the head. Concentrating, making decisions, remembering things.

She particularly hated the mornings. She would wake up too early in the morning and be unable to get back to sleep. So she would lie in the cool stillness of the morning beside her snoring husband and wish that she were dead. She would get her husband off to work and her daughter off to playschool and then she would go back to bed. Insomnia at night and a long, drugged nap in the afternoon. To get rid of some time. To escape into some other place that wasn't so cold and bleak. Then she would get up shortly before it was time to collect her daughter and she would try to make it look to her husband that she had done something during the day so that he wouldn't come home and shout at her again. But he always did. That's because most emotions are contagious. When you're around sad, angry or nervous people it's hard not to feel sad, angry or nervous yourself.

Depressions are one of the Three Great Poisons to marriage. The other two are alcohol and infidelity.

Eventually her husband spat the dummy. He took her off to her psychiatrist. He'd been through it all before. Into the clinic. They remembered her from her last two admissions. Lots of tears and emotional support as well as a carefully chosen anti-depressant medication. Then a three-week wait. Then some slow improvement in her mood. Not a fairy-tale ending but a slow emergence from the cave back into the light.

She knew the routine. It usually worked. One day she would find herself realising what a beautiful crisp autumn day it was. The next day John, one of her fellow patients, remarked that he hadn't heard her laugh before. But she had just found something funny. Some pleasure. She was coming to the edge of the desert.

Her psychiatrist pointed out her family tree. Her great-aunt had spent years in a psychiatric hospital and received ECT (electro-convulsive therapy or 'shock treatment') and her mother had been treated with anti-depressant medications over the years. There it was. Her depressive gene. Tumbling down the generations until it ended up in the ovum that was to become Anne.

As she improved she came to realise again how much her pain-in-the-neck husband had actually done for her. How much he cared. On another crisp autumnal day he took her home from the clinic to start again at home. No knight in shining armour. A man with a short temper and who snored. But he loved her and as she recovered she allowed herself to love him. Another start.

CASE HISTORY

John had been in the clinic with Anne. He had been improving well before she arrived. He enjoyed hearing her laugh. This woman with straggly hair and a haunted look in her eyes. Now she was brushing her hair and the spark had returned to her eyes.

It confronted him with what he'd been like when his sister had brought him to the clinic. It had been hard to convince him to stay since he 'knew' at the time that the clinic staff wanted to kill him. Yes, he'd been depressed. But he'd also tipped over the edge. He'd gone into a psychotic depression. His head was filled with delusions. Nasty ones. He had come to realise that his bowel was full of worms and that his heart had stopped. He told people that he had no legs, even though he walked around, albeit slowly. One day he had phoned his sister. 'I'm dead,' he said over and over again. Just as manic people believe that they are rich, famous and powerful, patients with psychotic depression believe that they are cursed, diseased, bankrupt. Even dead. His sister pushed the panic button and phoned his psychiatrist. He was down at the clinic in the blink of a haunted eye.

There had been a flurry of legal documents and a visit from a magistrate. John had been committed. Too depressed to give informed consent to the treatment that he needed, so the medical and legal professions got together and did what they had to. The next day he was taken into a room that smelled of crisp laundered sheets and given a general anaesthetic. He felt a little groggy and confused when he awoke a few minutes later. Using a computerised device, his psychiatrist had given him a two-second electric impulse across the right side of his forehead. His body had quivered a little as he had a highly controlled, electrically induced epileptic convulsion. Sounds a bit ghoulish doesn't it? A bit too One Flew Over The Cuckoo's Nest. But highly effective. John didn't crawl to the edge of the desert of depression. He was propelled there. He had ECT three times a week. After about eight treatments he began to emerge from his own cave of melancholy. The delusions dissipated. He heard Anne's laugh and it made him smile. There was hope.

Psychotic depression. Hell on earth. No time to muck around. Time to use that controversial treatment called ECT. If you haven't had it or administered it you can believe it's all hocus-pocus and the grandiose medical profession out of control. But if you know what it is and what it does you'll queue up for it if you have a treatment-resistant depression or a psychotic one. No one quite knows how it works. It just does.

CASE HISTORY

Michael was in the same clinic as Anne and John. Michael's depression had not responded well to his anti-depressant medication. He had tried three of them and they weren't working for him. One day he walked out of the clinic. He'd had enough.

Not far from the clinic was a tall bridge that carried six lanes of traffic across a stream. Passing motorists might have wondered what this hunched man was doing scurrying up the narrow pedestrian walkway. Michael stood at the top of the bridge for a moment before he jumped. He thought his life might flash before his eyes but it didn't. Just a single memory of when he was a kid and he used to dive off the high diving board at the public swimming pools. How frightened he'd been then. And how numbed he felt now. He raised his arms into the air as he had done on the diving board, just to impress his friends, and then he jumped into oblivion. It seemed to take minutes for him to hit the ground. There was a split second of shattering, jarring pain. And then he was dead.

Men do this. We hide away our emotional pain. The 'masked' depression. The 'smiling' depression. The surprise expressed by people when a man bursts into tears and can't stop crying. More surprise when he's found dead.

Michael's family were stunned. They talked about suing the psychiatrist. And the clinic. But then their anger turned to guilt and self-blame. They would face a long, hard grief. People who commit suicide are usually so tortured that they don't take into account the hurt that they will leave behind. They just want to stop their own torment. Whatever it takes.

QUESTIONS ABOUT DEPRESSION

These are the faces of depression. An awful, cruel illness. Focus on the last word. Illness. That's what this sort of depression is. Something goes wrong with the chemistry of your brain. That's why some, but not all, depressions require medications. So how do you tell which ones need the pills and which ones don't? You trot along to see your doctor and ask her, that's what you do. In order to know whether you need to play the patient game, check out the following questions.

❶ Do you feel sad, down, flat or tearful *most of the time*?
❷ Is it difficult for you to enjoy things or get pleasure out of things *most of the time*?
❸ Is it difficult to motivate yourself or feel enthusiastic?
❹ Do you want to withdraw from social interactions because it's just too difficult to talk to people?
❺ Is there a feeling of agitation, anxiety or dread that pervades your life?
❻ Do you feel 'fogged up' so that thinking, concentrating, paying attention, making decisions and your short-term memory are affected?

❼ Are you negative, disillusioned, critical and despairing? Do you beat yourself up too much or feel an inordinate sense of guilt or failure?

❽ Is your sleep pattern affected? Are you sleeping more or less than you usually do? In particular, do you wake up too early in the morning and find it difficult to get back to sleep?

❾ Ditto for your appetite. Are you eating more ('comfort eating') or less than you usually do?

❿ Is there one particular time of day when you consistently feel worse? (If this happens, it's usually the morning. Depressed people can almost feel human again by the evening but wake up the next day feeling dreadful again.)

⓫ Do you want to die?

If you answered these questions with more yeses than nos then you'd better get yourself down to the local quack. And at the risk of getting hate mail from my psychologist colleagues, I strongly suggest that this is *clinical depression* and is best treated by doctors. That doesn't mean to say that all you need is a prescription and everything will be rosy. Or that depressed patients should queue up for a few volts across the forehead. It just ain't that simple. Depressed people need a thorough assessment of their depression and a lot of emotional support to get through it.

Anti-depressant medications have their pitfalls. Keep in mind that:

♦ most of them have side-effects and the only way to work out whether you as an individual will get any side-effects is to give the drug a try and see what happens. If side-effects are intolerable then the answer is simple: try something else.

♦ all anti-depressants are created equal. They all have a thirty per cent failure rate. Even the super-duper you-beaut 'new' anti-depressants like Prozac fail to work thirty per cent of the time. That means that you sometimes have to try two or three anti-depressants before you find one that works well for you.

♦ they all take two to six weeks to start to work. That's why we call our customers 'patients'. . .

♦ there are three things that can go wrong with anti-depressants: they don't work (in thirty per cent of trials), they work partially (but there's a significant residue of depression) or they work well for a while, then they stop working (so that the patient finds himself drifting back into depression despite religiously taking the pills).

♦ when they work well, they work bloody well. Watching a patient recover from a deep depression is one of the most satisfying experiences in medical practice.

Q: So what causes depression?

A: There are two big groups of factors. I divide them into *biological* factors and *psychological* factors. The biological factors are things like those rotten genes that your parents gave you and the fact that you're drinking a bottle of Scotch a day. And the psychological factors? . . .

EXERCISE
_____

❶ Go down to your local bookstore.

❷ Ask them for my first book, entitled *Think Like A Shrink* (stop chortling!) . . .

❸ If they tell you they don't have it, punish them. Create a scene. Thump the counter. Hold your breath until you turn blue. Tell them to get it for you.

❹ Now find the part in it about the psychological factors that cause depression.

❺ Thanks. I've got a whole swag of kids at home and I could do with the royalties . . .

For those of you who are too mean to cough up the loot to buy my first book, I'll give you a sneak view of the psychological causes of depression. Most depressed patients find themselves in a situation that's *impossible*. There, simple isn't it? To get even more complex I believe that there are three roads to depression:

- the impossible stress
- the impossible need
- the impossible loss.

Want to know more? Then get off your chuff and get down to the bookstore, pronto . . .

H O W T O D E A L W I T H T H E D E P R E S S E D

Trot them down to talk to their local doctor. Talking may be the only thing they need but let the quack decide that. Sometimes a referral to a shrink is necessary. Once again, that's quack territory.

Never under-estimate how much support you can be to a depressed person. Or how much harm you can do. The *dos* are:

- *Do* take time to listen.
- *Do* take the person by the hand and organise to get competent professional help. Really depressed people can't make decisions and couldn't make a doctor's appointment even if they were standing in front of the receptionist. It's okay to be patronising in these circumstances.

The *don'ts* are:

- *Don't* try to diagnose and treat depression yourself just because you've read a few self-help books (like this one) and are a really caring person.
- If you've never experienced a severe, protracted depression before, *don't* presume that you have the

slightest idea of what the depressed person is experiencing. Friends and family members are often frustrated by their inability to 'cure' the patient's depression, so they project this frustration onto the Miserable One. They say 'all you have to do is pull your socks up' and 'you're just being weak and self-indulgent'. So the Miserable One becomes more miserable.

♦ *Don't* under-estimate the dangerousness of depression.

♦ *Don't* ignore your own depression because you believe it only happens to them and not you.

A final thought. I'd like to dedicate this section to a psychiatrist who was my first psychotherapy supervisor. A really nice bloke. One day his own depression got to him and he did a cruncher from a tall building. I saw his crumpled body in a photograph in the newspaper. Depression is such an ugly, brutal illness. And none of us is immune.

 The grief-stricken

I've tucked this section in behind the one on depression because, well, it seems logical. Depression and grief go hand in hand, but they're not the same thing. Grief is centred on loss. Grief is the process of mourning the loss of a person or thing. It's an understandable, unavoidable part of life and is (mostly) resolved after a few months. Depression, on the other hand, is stifling, pervasive and crippling. Grief is a process with a beginning, a middle and an end. Depression is a desert with no edges. Grief is part of the Human Condition. Depression is an illness. Grief is an affliction of the heart. Depression is an affliction of the soul. Get the drift?

LOSS

When you take a long, hard look at life, we human beings keep losing things. Not just car-keys and kids in shopping centres, but really important stuff, like our youth. To plagiarise Elizabeth Barrett Browning, let me count the ways that I lose thee . . .

❶ I lose that wonderful embracing world of the womb when I am painfully ejected through a pink tunnel into a cold world where my nasal passages are suctioned and my bottom is smacked by a person wearing a mask.

❷ I lose my position as the baby when the next sibling is born.

❸ I lose my youth, with its agility and freshness.

❹ I lose my naivety as I grow and realise that aspects of this world really suck. Like famine, war and Brussels sprouts.

❺ I lose my virginity. Even though it was becoming such a burden I can lose it only once and then I can never go back.

❻ I lose my lovers. For every ounce of pleasure in falling in love comes an ounce of pain when the affair ends.

❼ I lose my independence when I commit myself to someone in a relationship. It doesn't matter when I'm in the flurry of weddings and starting a new life. But it creeps in in the still of the night, years later, after we've had a huge row and I remember all those others who loved me when I was younger.

❽ I lose control of my children when they become pimply adolescents and tell me to nick off.

❾ I lose these same children a few years later when they leave home and try to be adults themselves. The home that was once so full and chaotic now seems to echo silence.

❿ I lose my power when I peak in my career and fresh-faced young Turks overtake me on the corporate ladder.

⓫ Around this time I start to lose people forever. A friend dies of cancer and another in a car accident. Then my parents die, one after the other in quick succession.

Then I have to scramble to save my marriage because my spouse is growing in a different direction and seems to be drifting away.

⓬ I lose confidence in my sexuality. I become menopausal. Or impotent.

⓭ I lose my health.

⓮ I lose my life.

So that's fourteen, but I'm still counting. Throw in the loss of a spouse who packs and goes one day. Add the loss of a child who is born but never breathes (which goes against the natural order: children are supposed to bury their parents). And then there was the redundancy, the bankruptcy and the fire that burned down the house and took the photograph album with it.

If we'd been warned about this we might never have been born.

Grief is something that gets us all, over and over again. Here's a case history about Michael's widow. The loss is, of course, death. But the process is similar whether it's loss of a job, an eye, a status, a foetus.

CASE HISTORY

Michael's wife Sarah was just getting ready to come to see him at the clinic when the phone rang. It was Michael's psychiatrist with the bad news. Michael had left the clinic and walked down to a nearby bridge where he had jumped to his death. Sarah thought for a split second that this was some sort of sick joke. For a split second. Then she knew it was true. She had feared it. To her Michael's depressive illness had always felt like swimming in shark-infested waters, never knowing when death would suddenly strike.

Her sense of loss had been like a dark ghost waiting in dusty corners to emerge. For a moment she was stunned. The psychiatrist seemed to be telling her things, muttering words of condolences, asking her questions. She could manage a syllable here or there but her mental world was scrambled. The shock would go on for many hours, even days. Even tomorrow morning she would awaken from her drugged sleep to the sense of numbness, hoping that it was all a bad dream but knowing it wasn't. Then the psychiatrist said, 'Can you get someone to bring you down here. I'll wait until you arrive.'

So there were mechanical phone calls to more stunned relatives, then there was a long drive to a place of disinfectant and sadness with a balding man in a suit trying to explain to her what happened. Sympathetic but clumsy young policemen. Tall, thin funeral directors who were a parody of themselves. Tearful faces and brief, sweet relief in embraces. A lot of well-intentioned people standing around not knowing what to say.

News reports said there were 'no suspicious circumstances'. Then the funeral and incense, the rehearsed passing words of understanding.

It was all a bit of a blur. Michael's ashes were scattered on a headland above the sea. It was raining, so the ashes didn't stay there very long. Before her very eyes what had been her husband became part of the earth once again. She hardly knew some of the people there. Then they went away and left a pile of flowers and white cards with silver writing. And the really hard work began.

Waves of anger and sadness. An aloneness that could never be expressed in words. The photos of him, the memories of him, the smell of his clothes. A great big hole in her life and a bed that was too big for one. Private tears, wept then gone, just like him. And just when she most needed people to be around they weren't there. It offended her that the world seemed to carry on, oblivious to the fact that Michael was no longer here. Shopkeepers still opened their shops. Skinny brown girls in bikinis still went to the beach. Laughter still erupted from the open windows of pubs. Didn't they know that Michael was dead?

It took Sarah a few months to begin to get over her grief. But it took her four years to feel that life was worth living and that she could ever trust another man to get close to her again. And how long did it take before Sarah was back to the way she was before Michael died? She never did. Not completely. People just don't ever fully recover from a loss as big as this.

Forty years later Sarah faces her own death. She remarried and had three kids. Now she is in a nursing home and the emphysema that has been draining her all these years is finally going to be her nemesis. And as she faces the inglorious, frightened gasping of her own dying her thoughts go back to Michael, as they have so often done over the years. And her hope that she might see him again soon.

So put away your hankies and let's get a grip on this thing called 'grief'. You know that you and I must both encounter it regularly, but we choose not to think about that too much. Denial is our oldest friend.

You see, grief is a predictable process. Check out the diagram.

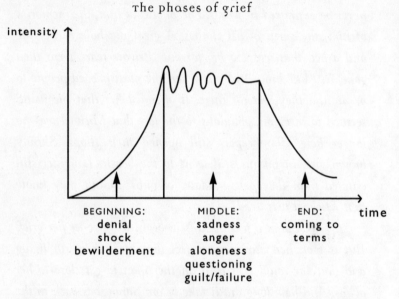

The phases of grief

There's a beginning, characterised by shocked, numbed bewilderment. No matter how much you prepare for grief you can't prepare for grief. Even if you know that your loved one is dying and the doctors are turning the life support machines off you can't prepare yourself for that last breath. To watch a person's life drain away before your eyes is a deeply moving experience. The stillness that settles on a corpse doesn't seem natural. Rest in peace, we say. To comfort ourselves. Because it confronts us with our own mortality and our knowledge that we're all running out of heartbeats.

Then there's a middle. In this phase of grief there's a lot of work to be done:

- waves of anger and sadness, just like Sarah experienced. The problem here is that there's no one to get angry at. Except doctors, but we're used to it. That's why we pay so much for our malpractice insurance. And who else is there to be angry at? God? Fate? Nature? Destiny? Ourselves, for having 'failed' this person and not kept them alive? All of the above. As you can see from the diagram, the 'waves' come thick and fast at first and then slowly ease off.
- a profound sense of aloneness. More tormenting than any physical pain.
- a need to understand. To get this loss into perspective. Why me? Why my family? Why?
- often there is a sense of failure, guilt or shame. If human beings can't find someone to blame then they usually blame themselves. Abused kids, for instance, always think that they must have done something to deserve being abused.

Then there's an end. Sort of. The line in the diagram never really returns to baseline. Perhaps a really significant loss, like a child or a spouse or a homeland is something that never ever goes away completely.

You must also understand that grief does two other things:

1 Grief *generalises*. That means that when you have too many losses at one time they all blur into one.
2 Grief *accumulates*. Every subsequent loss will confront you with the unfinished grief from previous losses.

consider this

Your father is dying. Slowly and surely of cancer. He's riddled with it and filled to the eyeballs with morphine. You want him to die so that he can be in peace but you also want him to live forever. Then your beloved cat goes under the wheels of a passing truck. When you scrape what's left of Kitty off the asphalt your thoughts are with the emaciated body of your dear old dad. You'll have to mourn for Kitty a bit further down the track. Right now you can hardly hold in your sadness concerning Dad. Kitty just confronts you with Dad. Grief generalises.

now consider this

Your father died last week. No more morphine but no more family dinners on Sunday and cheques to bail you out when you overspend on your credit card. At the funeral you are confused. With the sorrow about Dad comes a sorrow long forgotten. Your kid brother who was found dead in his cot when you were only eight years old. You didn't know what that feeling was then but you know now. Grief accumulates.

So how long should grief go on for? About three to six months should see most of it taken care of. A grief that persists severely for longer than a year is pathological. That usually means that it's stopped being grief and started being depression. It's stopped being a mood and started being an illness. The two overlap.

How to deal with the Grief-stricken

When someone you know is grieving, all you can do is let them know that you care and that you're there to help. Sometimes you can't say much more. If you listen to what people say to the widow at the graveside you'll understand that plenty of people put their foot into their mouths when they're trying to be consoling. They say, 'It's just as well he went so quickly at the end, dear.' That doesn't comfort the widow much at all. She's still all alone in the world. So extricate your *pied* from your *bouche* and just be there to hold her hand and hold her up when she sways.

Keep in mind that grief is a process. You can't hurry it. Don't try to 'make it all better again'. You'll end up sucking on leather.

And another thing. The hardest time for a bereaved person is often not the week after the loss, when the funeral occurs; people come from all over and the widow is propped up by all and sundry. No, the hardest time comes two or three months later when the grass is growing on the grave and all the proppers-up have gone away. That's the time you can show your compassion best of all.

Enough already with the grief. I'm getting sick of all this morbid stuff. Let's get on to something more lively. Like alcohol.

 # The Drunk

Back to the cocktail party. You remember. Skites, drunks, people trying to be clever. You're having a fun time chatting up a good-looking person who's been giving you the eye. Your hormones are rising when an argument about politics breaks out and someone calls someone else's wife 'fat' and the repartee that had been so much fun becomes an unpleasant scene of drunks with red faces and clenched fists.

Alcohol. Universally consumed nectar that can make our lives happy and sad. When alcohol goes right it's a lot of fun and when it goes wrong it's violence and intimidated children and blood on a steering wheel. And young women waking to feel exploited by the unknown, unclean, unshaven men who lie beside them.

CASE HISTORY

Simon liked a drop of wine. In fact he liked many drops of wine. Enough to fill his glass many times over. Before, during and after dinner. Every night of the week.

Simon was recognised by his friends as being a 'wine-snob' but he preferred the title 'connoisseur'. He talked about wines using a lot of silly terms. He called them 'naughty' and 'flippant' and 'decorous' and 'gallant' as if they were human beings. Half of the people in Simon's world thought he was so sophisticated and the other half thought he was a pretentious jerk. Simon listened only to the former group.

What they didn't realise was that Simon was an alcoholic. The wine-buff stuff was just a smoke-screen. Simon managed to put away at least a couple of bottles of wine every night. Careful never to drink before 5 p.m. Careful never to drink spirits or beer (so uncouth!). Careful never to be seen to sway or slur. One of those people who took pride in being able to hold their grog. But only because they'd drunk so much over so many years that their livers could metabolise it quick-smart. Always in control. But most of the time quietly drunk.

CASE HISTORY

Steve liked a drop of beer. In fact he liked bucketsful of the stuff. God, in his wisdom, had given Hindus their sacred cows, Catholics their holy water, Buddhists their golden icons and Steve, well God had given him beer.

Steve was 'blue collar', but not so vulgar as to go to the pub every night. That was for those grotty old drunks in dirty coats who smoked cigarettes right down to the filter. Steve just went there twice a week. Religiously. Pay night and Friday night. With the same group of mates. To have 'a few beers', or at least that's what he told Mrs Steve. But 'a *few' meant twenty. Mrs Steve knew that he would show up some time in the small hours of the following morning. He would be drunk and broke. The police might be involved. He was usually bleeding from somewhere. If he hadn't been in a punch-up he'd at least fallen over on some broken glass. She hated him when he was drunk. All her bitterness welled up. The black eyes he'd given her. The holiday money spent on a few 'shouts'. The loveless love-making taken by him so roughly while she diverted her face from the smell of his breath.*

Steve was an alcoholic. She knew that but he refused to know it. How had she got herself into this mess?

C A S E H I S T O R Y

Sean was a businessman. He was an alcoholic too but most people didn't know because they think of alcoholics as being Steves, not people who wear blue business suits with starched white shirts and red ties. Sean 'did lunch' a lot. He liked the idea of The Firm buying his grog. He also liked the bar fridge in the boardroom. He liked 'happy hour' on Friday evenings. Once he plied his new secretary with alcohol and then had sex with her on the boardroom table after everyone else had left. She resigned shortly after that. A little older and wiser.

Sean never got too plastered at work. He waited until he got home, then he hit the whisky bottle. He made sure that his mobile phone was turned off and his answering machine was on. There was no one else at home. His wife had taken the kids and left several years ago. He didn't want to have her whinge in the public arena of the divorce court about his drinking so he just signed everything over to her and didn't press for access to the children. He was now at the point where he had to either sober up or die.

He tried Alcoholics Anonymous once or twice but said that he couldn't identify with the 'higher power' stuff since the nuns had beaten any godliness out of him at school. But that was just a convenient excuse. Then he tried to drink only light beer but found that he could drink gallons of it and get just as pissed as he did on whisky. Then his doctor warned him that he was incubating a severe case of cirrhosis of the liver. That's when your liver is so damaged and so scarred by all the toxic insults you've thrown at it over the years that it curls up its hepatic toes and refuses to work.

Sean's work performance had been going downhill. The boss was on the point of ditching him when he stopped showing up for work. Not just another bender. He'd died in his bed at home of a stomach ulcer that had ruptured and spilled acid and blood into his abdomen. Even the hardened ambulance officers were disgusted at his state. He'd been dead for three days. Rigor mortis had set in. His flat was filthy and his bedroom floor covered in vomit and faeces.

DEFINING ALCOHOLISM

These are the faces of alcoholism. The constant drinker, like Simon, who never seemed drunk but drank so much that his liver became the colour of cowardice. Just like the French do. They drink wine with most meals, they don't stagger or slur, but they die of alcoholic cirrhosis. Then the binge drinker, like Steve. They often rot their brains. Keep in mind that alcohol is the third most common cause of dementia. What's dementia? That's when you lose your marbles. No thought, no memory, no mental processes, just confusion and a vegetating life.

Then there's Sean, who highlights the fact that alcoholics can be beautiful, successful people. Not necessarily drunks in bus shelters.

So how do you define alcoholism? How much grog is too much?

All sorts of learned people have tried to do this. Like the World Health Organisation, the American Psychiatric Association and the National Institutes of Mental Health. Now here's Dunn's version of the definition of alcoholism. It's fiendishly simple really. There are just three criteria: you drink too much, you get into trouble and you can't control it. Say that again?! . . . All right:

❶ You drink too much. For men that means no more than forty grams of alcohol per day and for women just half that. (Sorry, ladies, but the boffins lay down these rules, not me.) So how much does that mean in terms of hard liquor? As a rule of thumb, a 'standard drink' equals ten grams of alcohol. A 'standard drink' is a nip of spirits, a glass of wine or a 250 ml glass of beer. So depending upon your genitalia, multiply these amounts by two or four.

❷ You get into trouble. With your spouse. With your boss. With the police. With your doctor. With your bank manager. Excessive, compulsive alcohol consumption just causes trouble.

❸ You can't control it. You just think you can. 'Not a problem, doc' you say as you leave your doctor's office. You're good for the first two weeks. Then you get complacent. Then you 'bust'. Then you're a drunk again. I don't believe that anyone is really beginning to sober up until they've been alcohol-free for six months. And that's a minimum. Just a start too. When you get to this point it's clever to keep the old AA axiom in mind: 'One day at a time'. That means that you don't have to face the prospect of remaining sober for the rest of your life, just today. Each morning you wake up and say 'I'm going to remain sober today'. Then tomorrow you do the same thing. And the day after. And the day after. Pretty soon you're really old and still have your marbles.

THE DRUNK'S FAMILY

A word for the children of alcoholics. You're a downtrodden lot. You face similar issues:

- ♦ It's so much easier if Dad falls over drunk in the corner of the living room than in the street. When Dad falls over in the street the whole family must confront the shame.
- ♦ Dad's alcoholism becomes a 'dirty secret' for the family. The neighbours all know damned well that he's a hopeless drunk but we have to keep up pretences. Often to protect Mum's fragile pride.
- ♦ Dad sets the emotional tone for the family. You all work around him. When he comes home you have to walk on eggshells around him so that you can find out what sort of mood he's in. If he's a happy drunk, you can relax. If he's an angry drunk you have to stay out of his way. If he's a sad drunk you have to soothe him. If he's a philosophical drunk you have to sit and listen to all the boring stories and reminiscences you've heard a hundred times before.
- ♦ It's hard enough facing the violence of television but it's horrible facing the violence in the living room. All children of alcoholics can tell stories of sitting in the dark outside their parents' bedroom listening to them shout at each other.
- ♦ You're supposed to get more uptight when you get closer to school. But you know the feeling when school becomes

an oasis and your anxiety level increases as you walk home.
Something wrong with that.

♦ Finally, you know that you've colluded with your father's
alcoholism. You've gone down to the shop to buy him some
grog just to shut him up. There are times when it's easier on
everyone if he's drunk in the corner than annoying people
in his sobriety, like a bear with a sore head.

HOW TO DEAL WITH THE DRUNK

Drunks rely heavily on three very primitive defences: denial,
rationalisation and projection. They don't think that they're
alcoholics. If they acknowledge that they're drinking too much
they'll always find someone or something to blame. It could never
be *their* fault. That's why they're also good at 'doing geographicals'.
That's when you blame your drinking on the place where you're
living. So you shift somewhere else. Then you start drinking again.
So you blame *that* place. So you shift again, and so on.

If you're a drunk then you've got to accept that this is *your*
problem and the only one who can do anything about it is *you*. I
strongly recommend that you try to develop a relationship with
your local chapter of Alcoholics Anonymous. It's your best chance.

If you're the loved one of a drunk then get yourself along to a
meeting of Alanon. That's the loved one's equivalent of AA. You'll
hear a lot of stories and learn a lot of tricks there. The most
important message that you must take away is that *you can't rescue your
beloved drunk*. Only he can. So sometimes the best thing you can do
is to stop fantasising that you can heal him. Do the reverse: withdraw
all support. Leave him if needs be. Sometimes alcoholics have to get
a lot worse before they get better. When they wake up in the gutter
covered in their own urine and vomit it's hard for them to carry on
their denial. That's when you can get to them: when they're in crisis.
But sometimes you have to 'engineer' the crisis first.

So don't just sit there reading. Go out and organise a crisis . . .

The Infertile

So you're back at the cocktail party. You don't want to be classified as a drunk so you're counting your grams. Of alcohol, that is. Trouble is you've drunk just about sixty, so wind back on the intake or your kids will end up leaving you in a gutter somewhere.

You strike up a conversation with a woman who's there with her handsome husband. The talk turns to children. You ask how many children she has. She replies 'None'. You ask 'Why?' and then make some crass comment about how clever she is to have made it this far in life without being burdened by a couple of brats and how lucky she must be to have this lifestyle of freedom and cocktail parties. Suddenly she bursts into tears and excuses herself. Mr Handsome hurries away after her. You're left stunned, holding your next ten grams in your hand, and wondering what you've just said. On your tongue is the faint taste of leather and you realise that you must have made some extraordinary shoe-in-mouth gaff. Everyone nearby stops talking and for an agonising moment you're left there, wishing that the lawn would open, swallow you and then close over as if you'd never been there.

A few moments later Mr Handsome comes back to collect their bags and coats. He explains hurriedly as he passes by that they've actually been trying to have children for a number of years now, but without success. You see the look in his eye. They'd trade all the parties in the world for a baby. A child to call their own. You look down in clumsy shame.

You've just fallen into a trap that most people fall into at some stage. Failing to understand the distress of the Infertile. Saying things that you think are helpful or funny but just rubbing salt into their wound. So why is it that infertility is so painful? Because it's connected intimately with one of our Two Reasons for Being. Number one is to stay alive. Number two is to keep the species alive. Infertile people must face a lifelong sentence of being unable to satisfy an absolutely primeval instinct. They have an itch they can't scratch. And unless you've encountered infertility first-hand it's easy to under-estimate just how pain-full these people are.

CASE HISTORY

Penelope wasn't infertile. Her husband David was. Of course Penelope didn't know that when she married him. She presumed, as we all do, that they would have no problems with making babies. Their life was organised and planned. Career path, superannuation, upward mobility, long-range goals, time management. Penelope and David were good at that stuff. Then David's testicles got in the way. They weren't doing their job. Sure, they were pouring out hormones so that David had hair on his chest, a baritone voice and a twinkle in his eye when she wore that frilly thing. But hardly any sperms. And the ones that he did manage to produce in the 'collection room' at the lab were on their last legs. Or tails as the case may be.

They found out about David's deficiencies in the sperm department many years after they'd married. They had the house and cars. He'd got that promotion. The bank manager was looking favourably upon them. Time to make babies. Just an heir, not a litter. Or perhaps a pigeon-pair boy-and-girl arrangement (in that order). But it was not to be.

After a year of 'trying' Penelope went off to see the doctor. Needless to say David was roped in on this pretty soon afterwards and introduced for the first time to the 'collection room'. He was thankful that it had the security of a lock on the door that he could secure from the inside. He'd had too many nosy shop assistants at the menswear department 'pop in' on him when he was in the dressing rooms . . .

The doctor was grim-faced when he delivered the news. Half a dozen sperms that looked as if they had gout. Not enough to make babies. The only good news was that he would never have to have a vasectomy . . .

The couple were shattered. This wasn't in the Grand Plan. David had an immense sense of failure. Here was a piece of paper from a laboratory that questioned his very manhood. All those other manly things he could do. Play rugby. Satisfy a woman. Hammer a nail in straight. Read maps. Parallel park. But not this. He couldn't be a father.

There followed a long process of healing. 'Long' here means years. A grief to work through. Shock, numbness, bewilderment. Waves of anger and sadness. The unspoken but deep disappointment felt by Penelope and the guilt felt by David. And the isolation. The extraordinary sense of isolation.

Adult human beings became divided into the fertile and the infertile. The fertile group had no idea of the agonies borne by the infertile group. The infertile group fell together to support each other. Huddled in the waiting rooms of infertility clinics. The infertile group changed channels on the TV every time the nappy ads came on. And hid in their houses on Mother's Day and Christmas Day. The infertile group bought kittens and puppies to try to ease their yearning. The infertile group tried to hold back their tears and confusion when people felt entitled to ask them about when they were going to have kids. 'You can have one of ours' the fertile people would say, trying to be funny. The fertile group envied the infertile group their disposable income, their restaurant dinners and overseas trips. The infertile group envied the fertile group their baby photos, their tuck shop duty at school, their sense of family. They would give up every aspect of their lifestyle, they would live in a hovel on the wrong side of the tracks, just to have a baby.

But just before you pull your hankies out again, let me tell you that Penelope and David's story had a happy ending. Donor sperm. Some faceless university student with reasonable genes had gone to the infamous 'collection room' and rescued them with a few dirty thoughts and a well-rehearsed technique. Sure, David had to come to terms with the fact that he would never be the biological father to his child but when Penelope brought forth a beautiful baby girl he knew that he would love this child forever.

CONSEQUENCES OF INFERTILITY

And there you have it. The agonies of infertility. Infertile couples go through a number of predictable emotional consequences to their predicament. Here's the list:

- ♦ grief. In fact every time an infertile woman menstruates she discovers yet another sense of loss. I have encountered a number of infertile women who have gone to gynaecologists and told a whole lot of lies about their heavy menstruation in order to get a hysterectomy. If thy womb offends thee, pluck it out . . .
- ♦ alienation. Infertile people feel different. They've been marginalised from the mainstream of civilisation. They look like us, they speak like us, but they're fringe dwellers. In business suits and twin-sets and pearls. They're in the out-club.

- avoidance. Later on in this book you'll encounter another group of Pain-full People who have suffered a trauma and will do anything they can to avoid the trauma. The Infertile will avoid any reminder of their infertility. These are the people you'll see shopping in the all-night supermarket rather than go during the day when the mothers are there with their toddlers.
- sex and sexuality. Nothing is more fun than bonking in an attempt to conceive. It just seems so natural. So intimate, so loving. Two people complimenting each other by offering to share their genes forever. It's time for candlelight and poetry and that wee lacy thing. Now you know what infertile people miss out on. They even question their own manliness or womanliness.
- guilt/failure. Speaks for itself.
- depression. Not just grief. This is a cruel grief that goes on and on. With every menstruation. With every failed attempt and every painful, intrusive surgical procedure. Never knowing when to give up. Never knowing when it will end. It comes as no surprise that infertile people get well and truly depressed. A colleague of mine did a study on women attending an in vitro fertilisation clinic and found that *twenty-two per cent of the female patients were clinically depressed.*

Finally, a word about the concept of 'psychogenic infertility'. Infertility affects one couple in seven and about twenty per cent of these couples will apparently have no diagnosable cause for their failure to breed. Some doctors have questioned whether some patients can bring about their own infertility by subconsciously not wanting to get pregnant. I find this whole idea very fascinating, but very dangerous. My fascination stems from my slow 'conversion' over the years from being very sceptical about 'psychosomatic' theories to now being much more tolerant. On the other hand the danger in these theories lies in the tendency for the Infertile to blame themselves anyway, so notions of 'psychogenic infertility' simply serve to increase the self-contempt experienced by these poor people. And where does the truth lie in this debate? Who knows? The jury is still out on this one . . .

HOW TO DEAL WITH THE INFERTILE

First, keep your foot a long way from your mouth. If you have a friend or loved one who is battling with this nasty problem, be aware that infertile people are very sensitive about the issue. So go easy on the tactless jokes and offering unsolicited advice, which is only patronising and only serves to trivialise their pain.

Infertile people need comfort and understanding. If they must hide away at Christmas, let them. They may take years to get through this ordeal. Don't be precious and drag them to family events if they don't want to come. In their own way and in their own time they'll heal and then get back to some semblance of normality again. But for many this is one of those griefs that never quite goes away.

 # The Twin

Now here's more of the truth-is-stranger-than-fiction stuff. I'm going to tell you the saga of a number of patients I encountered while working at a psychiatric hospital. The case histories describe real people. Of course to protect their identity I won't name them. And also to stop any of them suing the pants off me.

CASE HISTORY

Number 1 was a 28-year-old woman who liked to swallow fish-hooks. She was admitted to the medical ward of the psychiatric hospital to see whether she would be able to 'pass'* them or whether she'd need surgery to fish (pardon the pun) them out.

Number 1 had had years of this. Whenever she felt needy or unable to cope she just swallowed fish-hooks. Bizarre self-inflicted injury. Anything to be a patient. Tucked up in bed in a regressed child-like role. Inadequacy taken to its most absurd extreme. Even when she was well she was never too well. A bit dependent, a bit provocative, a bit passive-aggressive. A bit of a pain in the backside in fact.

CASE HISTORY

Number 2 was a similarly obnoxious woman. She was ostensibly admitted because of depression but then she went about provoking and annoying all the staff and all the other patients. Often regressed, silly, over-familiar then antagonistic. Hard work.

She was eventually discharged although that was quite an effort. She'd decided that she liked being a patient. Not long after discharge she committed suicide by jumping from the roof of her boarding house.

---

* In this instance 'pass' is a medical euphemism for being able to poo them out without them getting stuck anywhere sensitive . . .

Number 3 was a self-mutilator. She'd go into an inexplicable spiralling sense of dissociation. That means that she would feel detached from her body, her environment would seem unreal and unfamiliar and she would feel detached from any sense of herself and her identity. Then she'd take something sharp and cut herself. If she had to, she'd break a bottle or mirror and use the glass from that. She would have to see her own blood. Don't ask me why, but it made her feel real again. It wasn't about pain or trying to kill herself. She just needed to be brought down from the spiral of dissociative discomfort.

I thought she might be able to find something a little less, shall we say, dramatic to do when she reached these regular crises. So I taught her how to insert an acupuncture needle into her hand. It didn't work. Because it didn't make her bleed. So she used the needle to impale the veins on the back of her hand. That worked.

Number 4 tried to commit suicide by hitting herself over the head with a rock. How weird is that?! Her boyfriend had just jilted her and she could find no reason to live. She was brought to the hospital late at night by the police who'd found her wandering the city streets with a huge bruise on her forehead. For her own safety she was committed. Psychiatric hospitals don't really have padded cells. But they do have 'seclusion rooms' where patients who are out of control can be locked away, usually with a chemical strait-jacket, i.e. a whole lot of sedatives on board. Let's not get wishy-washy here. Some patients just don't respond to TLC and cajoling. Hence the room with unbreakable windows and a lock on the door.

Number 4 spent the night in the seclusion room bashing her fists on the door and screaming at the top of her lungs. By morning it was all over. Her wounds could be dressed and she could be tidied up a little before she was sent home. But on condition that she'd come back to talk to her psychiatrist and leave the rocks in the quarry. Where they belong.

CASE HISTORY

Number 5 was a woman who was overweight and rather plain. So call me what you want, but she was a hard woman to like. Not just her appearance but her huge attitude problem.

She presented herself to the hospital seeking admission. There didn't seem to be a lot of reason to spend thousands of taxpayers' dollars by admitting her so she was sent away. Shortly after this a passing motorist phoned the hospital to say that a fat woman with a scowl on her face was lying across the road outside the hospital, stopping traffic. Moments later the police arrived at the hospital with Number 5 in tow. What to do now? Should she be treated as a patient or a law-breaker? The police didn't want to charge her so she became a patient. She knew how to get her way . . .

The policed returned to the hospital three days later. Number 5 had mailed her bank manager a letter. Scrawled in

*childish writing across a dirty piece of paper were the words
'put $100 000 into account number 4569-98345-1221 or
you are dead meat . . . ' Number 5 was so chaotic in her
thinking that she didn't even know how to rob a bank. She'd
written her own account number down. Tracing her was a piece
of cake. The constables rolled their eyes and sternly advised her
never to do it again.*

CASE HISTORY

*Number 6 was a charming and warm woman whose seductive
exterior hid the tortured rage that she'd carried all her life. She
was a shrew. Unpredictable in her emotions. Shallow and
manipulative. Delightful one minute, mocking the next. She came
to hospital because she'd cut her wrists. Not just in the privacy of
her own home. No, Number 6 needed desperately to be noticed.
So she stood in the centre of a busy downtown plaza and did it
there. Just as all the office workers were perching on park benches
to eat their lunchtime sandwiches. Talk about attention. She got
plenty of it. Do-gooders rushing to help. Sirens. Police. Ambulance
paramedics. Newspaper reporters. The works.*

So why am I telling you this? What did all these women have in
common? Let's get to the point here.

The point is that all these patients:

♦ were female
♦ were twins
♦ had a female co-twin
♦ were highly personality-disordered. Almost to the point of
  insanity. And mostly with that dreaded entity, the
  Borderline Personality Disorder.

And was this all just coincidence? I doubt it. I've seen it many more times since I collected this *cohort* of patients. Disturbed women who are twins and have a female co-twin. I don't know why, but this seems to be a toxic recipe. Furthermore I've searched the world medical literature to try to find anyone else who's described this good-twin, bad-twin phenomenon previously. But I can't. No one else seems to have noticed this association before.

This doesn't mean that all sets of female twins contain one right nutter in the pair. But when the nutter is there, she's really nuts. And another thing. The co-twin seems to have consistently turned out very well. Nice, mature, integrated women with sanity and stability in their lives. Like yin and yang. While their sisters were off the wall. Why should this be? I have my theories, but they're a bit too esoteric to go into here. They're all about the development of a sense of self. This is a life task that confronts us all as we grow. But for twins it's a whole lot harder. Their sense of themselves is diluted by the presence of this other person who shares their birthdays and their lives. And for some female twins it becomes impossible. So they grow up twisted.

Don't ask me why males seem to be unaffected. They just do.

HOW TO DEAL WITH THE TWIN

If you're a twin (and one birth in eighty will be twins) then you don't necessarily have to panic over these observations. You already know the pleasures and pains of twinship. It's nice to be different and to get some extra attention because of your twinship. But it's also important for you and your twin to each have a separate identity.

A message for parents: it's fair enough to dress them up the same from time-to-time as long as it doesn't look like too much of a freak-show. That's all about the specialness of twinship. But it's also important for your twins to develop a sense of individuality.

So they do best if they have their own hairstyle and their own clothes and their own friends, interests, etc.

The trick is in getting the balance right.

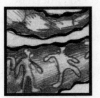 # The psychotic

Everyone knows what psychotic people are. They're axe-wielding murderers, right?

Wrong. Sorry, but most axe-wielders are actually sane. Nasty types, but sane nevertheless. That's just the Hollywood version of the Psychotic. Now I'm going to give you a crash course on psychosis. What it is and how it affects people. You'll see that it's got little to do with the Hallowe'en movies. It's got more to do with cruel mental illnesses that rob sufferers of years of their lives. And don't get complacent. Schizophrenia and manic-depression* each ensnare about one person in 120 at some time in their lives. So I'd take a guess and say that maybe one person in forty is going to get some sort of psychosis at some time in their lives. So pay attention. This could be you. Or your kids.

First some concepts. A patient with a psychosis develops characteristic signs and symptoms, just as with any other illness:

♦ delusions. They're fixed, false beliefs. Like being followed everywhere you go by CIA agents who look just like

---

* I use the old term 'manic-depression' in this section. There's a trend afoot to rename this illness Bipolar Affective Disorder, or BAD for short. I prefer the former. It's like calling a spade a spade and a manic a manic.

passers-by. Or being poisoned or being the Pope. Presuming you're not really the Pope, that is. Psychotic people believe firmly in their delusions. You can't convince them otherwise. If the CIA is following them then, dammit, there's no way that you're going to be able to convince them otherwise.

♦ hallucinations. Everyone knows what they are. People who take LSD get them and so do fervently religious people when they're in an ecstatic trance. Delirious people get them when, say, they've got a high fever or brain infections. And so do psychotics. But psychotics get more auditory hallucinations than visual ones. That's what they refer to when they talk about 'the voices'. They're voices in their heads. Mocking them. Laughing at them. Talking about them. Telling them to do things. Like to kill themselves. As you can see, most psychotic hallucinations are no fun.

♦ thought disorder. That means that their thoughts get all jumbled up. In psychiatry we have all sorts of quaint terms to describe just how jumbled. Terms like *tangentiality, over-inclusion, derailment, circumlocution* and *knight's-move*. They speak for themselves.

♦ emotional instability. Psychotics characteristically go through highs and lows. If you're a manic-depressive then the highs are through the roof and the lows are through the floor.

♦ psychosocial deterioration. You start life as an accountant. Then you go mad. Then you become a bank teller. Then you become a clerk in the public service. Then you become a labourer. Then you become unemployed. Then you become a pensioner. That's psychosocial deterioration. Psychosis eats away at your personality. At your ability to relate to people and organise your life. At your ambition and enthusiasm. There aren't too many high-flying psychotics.

Now these are gross generalisations. Not all psychotics have them all. Some people will be lucky enough to have one or two psychotic episodes and then fully recover. Don't ask me how often that happens. I see only the sick ones. Like George and Graham.

CASE HISTORY

George went mad in his early twenties. Slowly at first, but then he picked up momentum and really went off his tree. He ended up being taken to hospital in the back of a police wagon. He'd been found sitting on a bench in a railway station talking to himself. Or so it seemed. He was actually talking to 'the voices'. He was pretty dirty and unkempt and he'd taken to wearing three pairs of shoes at any one time, starting with a pair of the right size, then a bigger pair and then a pair of real clod-hoppers. He told the police that that was to prevent the electricity from entering him through his feet, coming up through his body and 'flashing' in his brain. That had happened often. Before he took to the Goofy-style footwear, that is.

So how had this figure of pathos ended up here? Hunched in the back of a paddy-wagon and muttering to himself. A head full of voices, jabbering to each other. Talking about him. Holding a running commentary of what he was doing and what he was thinking. How had this person's life become so chaotic?

Four years previously he'd been a pretty clean-cut eighteen-year-old who worked as a pastrycook's apprentice and entertained escapist fantasies of spending his life in a little hut by the sea. One night he smoked some marijuana at a party and became agitated and withdrawn. He'd told no one, but the dope had started the voices. Not that dope drives you mad, it just brings out the madness that's hiding there.

Then he began to make mistakes at work. Silly mistakes. He couldn't concentrate. When he filled a batch of chocolate eclairs with banana ice-cream one day his boss had had enough and George found himself without a job.

Then he couldn't sleep so he got into the pattern of sleeping all day and staying awake all night. That suited him because he could go through life watching late-late movies on TV and never having to interact socially with anyone. Because talking to people was just so hard. He felt as if he didn't have anything to say. That's when he realised that he had a hole in his brain. He just knew. The hole was so big that he had more hole than brain. And there were people in the hole. They were talking to him. Not just when he smoked dope now, but during his every waking hour. Life was getting harder.

George took to washing himself every other day. Then that turned into once a week. Perhaps. If he could be bothered. He got pretty depressed too. Then he was thrown out of the flat he shared with two others, ostensibly because he couldn't pay the rent. But they wanted him out at all costs. He'd become too weird. So he ended up in a boarding house and on the dole.

The grumpy old woman who ran the boarding house knew exactly what was wrong with George. He was a schiz. She'd had no medical training but she could spot them a mile off. She had another four or five of them in the boarding house already. When the local mobile psychiatric team came to visit her other *schizes she got them to check out George. One look and a two-minute chat was enough. Would George like to have some treatment and follow-up for his mental illness? No, he would not, thank you very much. George didn't want a bar of these intrusive people in their jeans and sneakers pushing their pills at him. They could stick it. So he packed up his bag and took his hollow brain and his voices to another boarding house. But he was picked up by the police before he got too far. His flatmates had been right. He was too weird.*

And now he was here at the sprawling red-brick psychiatric hospital in the outer suburbs. Being pumped full of drugs and made to have a good scrub in a hot bath. Of course he hated it. Every interminable moment of it. But after a few weeks his head was starting to come right. Not perfect, mind you, but a little less scattered. And a little less weird.

Trouble was he was left with the 'chronic' symptoms of schizophrenia. Pills are good at making the voices a little quieter and the paranoia a little more manageable. But they're no good at getting a schizophrenic to be able to concentrate, plan, manage his finances and relate to people. George insisted upon discharge and there was no legal way for the hospital to deny his request. So off he went. He stopped his medication the moment he left and it was only a couple of months before he was back. The hole in his brain was back and so were the voices. And the shoes. And the stench.

George became one of those severe, chronic schizophrenics who spend their lives going into and out of hospital. They're called 'revolving door' patients. For obvious reasons.

And that's the sad and sorry tale of George. Now let's get into something more lively: Graham's manic-depression.

C A S E   H I S T O R Y

One day Graham went high. Out of the blue. Sort of. He'd had those two depressions in the past but he'd never even recognised how depressed he'd been. So he just 'weathered' them until they went away. Each depression lasted about six months. A year of his life down the drain. But now, now Graham was into something different. Happiness. Unbridled and breathless. A life of it. Happiness pervading every aspect of his existence. Graham had become manic.

It began at work. He was a motor mechanic. Not a bad one either. He liked BMWs and high-octane petrol and grease up to his elbows. When it started his workmates noticed that he was speaking quickly, not working a lot and being sort of strange. Like smearing grease in hieroglyphics down the side of a Toyota van. That sort of strange.

Then he went missing. He came back saying that he'd just had to go home to have sex with his wife. Yes, she'd been just as surprised. The boss was not amused. Graham smelt of beer. He was sent home with the message to tidy his act up or face the sack. The sack came the next day. Graham made a pass at a female customer who had slapped his face. That was enough for the boss, who liked Graham but couldn't afford to lose customers.

The boss spoke to Mrs Graham. Was Graham all right? What did she think of his recent behaviour. A phone call to Mrs Graham's GP. He came down to the house that evening.

Graham was pretty high by then. Only a few hours sleep in the past six days. Now he was talking gibberish. Fast gibberish. Something about being 'God's Chosen One'. Interspersed with lots of laughter. How would Graham like to be referred to a psychiatrist? Couldn't care less, doc, and might I say what an absolutely spiffing and talented man you are. Here, have my wife for the night. By now the good doctor and Mrs Graham knew that there was something very, very wrong with Graham. Off to the clinic in the middle of the night. Interviews, pills, side-effects, complaints, then resignation and a clearing of the manic chaos of his head.

Unlike George, Graham responded well. He developed full insight into his illness and a motivation to stay well. He even took his lithium faithfully. Anything to avoid slaps across the face and trips to psychiatric clinics. Manic-depressives often do well. They have a better overall prognosis than schizophrenics. So if God appears before you and tells you that you must suffer either schizophrenia or manic-depression but you can choose, choose manic-depression.

Take these case histories as being fairly gross. Not all schizophrenics hang out in railway stations and not all manic-depressives write hieroglyphics in grease. The themes are there. These are the two most common forms of psychosis. There are plenty more. Some are really odd, but this section is for education, not ghoulish curiosity. Keep in mind that there's nothing romantic about madness. These are the most pain-full of all people.

Schizophrenics have prominent delusions, 'voices', jumbled thoughts and psychosocial deterioration. From accountant to pensioner. Manic-depressives have more mood component. 'High' times are whoopee a bongo let's party you horrible poo-faced bores. 'Lows' are oh my god is this all I've got to look forward to for the rest of my crestfallen God forsaken life. If at all possible, go through life avoiding them both.

How to deal with the Psychotic

Seek professional help as quickly as your dialling finger will summon it. A good place to start is your GP. Don't under-estimate the distress that psychotic people suffer. Ten per cent of schizophrenics commit suicide.

Even psychologists won't whinge if I say that psychosis is a medical problem. Drugs. We doctors prefer the snooty title 'medications'. Deride them as much as you like, they're still the cornerstone of the treatment of psychosis. Granted, they're not very pretty drugs. Sort of heavy-duty, sedating, trembling, mouth-drying actually. But given some time and dosage adjustment most people can put up with them.

Don't try to treat psychotics with sympathy and herbal tea.

 The mistress

Princess Di summed it up wonderfully in her famous 'go for broke' TV interview. There were three people in her marriage, she said, and that was one too many. So this is a chapter about extra-marital affairs. More specifically a chapter about The Other Woman. You'll soon see that TOW is a perfect blend of the Painful (wanton, home-wrecking, scarlet woman) and the Pain-full (lonely, powerless, trapped). And yes, there is a moral to the story: an affair is an arrangement where three people end up getting hurt.

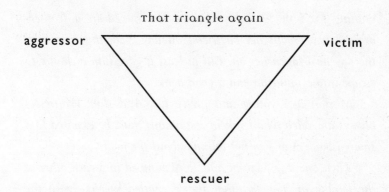

That triangle again

aggressor   victim

rescuer

Funny things, triangles. Or at least triangular relationships. You will recall from the section on the Professional Victim and the Compulsive Rescuer that when three people end up together they usually relate in the predictable way: there's a persecutor (or aggressor), a victim and a rescuer. Keep that in mind as you read the tragic tale of Marian the Mistress.

CASE HISTORY

Marian met Tony at work. No, she wasn't his secretary and he wasn't a businessman in the middle of his mid-life crisis. She was actually a waitress at a coffee shop and he liked to go there for a quiet cappuccino and a chance to bury his head in a book and have some 'time out'. He'd gone there maybe ten times before they started chatting, although he'd noticed her the first time he'd set foot in the place. He wondered later on, when the affair was in full swing, whether he'd decided to keep going back because of her. Yes, he'd decided, that's exactly what had happened.

He was in his later thirties, a jeweller by trade. He had a shop nearby. He'd become so bored with it that he'd hired a young female assistant. She was young and pretty but did nothing for him. Probably because she talked in a feather-brained way about her boyfriend all day. Sometimes he rued the day he'd taken her on. But at least it gave him a chance to escape into cappuccino and a good book.

Marian was young and pretty too. And slim. Waitresses always are. Men who work in restaurants must be exposed to a smorgasbord. And I'm not talking about the food.

Then one day Marian and Tony bumped into each other at the local gym. The fact that they'd chatted previously in the coffee shop made it easy to sit down and chat together on a bench surrounded by bars, dumb-bells and muscle-bound freaks.

There was a chemistry. It helped that she was wearing a lot of skin-hugging lycra. He could see her slim figure while trying not to stare. She'd been gyrating to the calls of an anorectic woman with a ghetto blaster and a microphone. He'd been doing the male equivalent: pumping iron. They seemed to have a lot in common. They chatted for half an hour. The gym was having its Christmas party soon. He encouraged her to go. He was hungry for her time and attention. She was curious. He was cute, as women say, but she suspected that he was married and she had no interest in becoming entwined in an extra-marital affair. Or at least that's what she thought that day as she left the gym.

She arrived at the Christmas party late. She was with some other women and they'd all had too much to drink. He'd almost given up hope. He homed in on her like a heat-seeking missile. That night began with just a kiss. But lots more chemistry. Hormones too. He was being pushy and she didn't mind. They sort of fell together in a motel room. That's how we get the word 'mistress'. It's half-way between a 'mister' and a 'mattress' . . .

On this first night there was no talk of his being married but she sort of knew. But after that night she couldn't get him off her mind. He'd been charming. And terrific in bed. She yearned to see him again.

He phoned. He came to the coffee shop every day. He sent flowers. The affair was on.

Her fears that he was married were confirmed when she asked for his home phone number. 'I'd prefer if you didn't ring me there. You see, I'm married. Well, at least for now.'

It came as no surprise but it was still a crushing disappointment. She tried to look on the bright side. She needed him. She needed his touch and his love-making. She became dizzy when he showed up at the coffee shop. Heart–genital love. Lots of it.

She'd play it by ear, she decided. Perhaps this was something that she could handle. He wouldn't clutter up her life. He wouldn't become clingy as young, needy men became. He wouldn't threaten her own need for independence. He wouldn't drive her away with his dependence. There was something comfortable in the way he would get out of her bed and the door would close after him. After all he didn't need her; he had a wife. Wife. She tried not to think about his wife.

Then she found out he had two small daughters. She tried not to think about them either.

She just took it as it came. She worked within the rules. He could ring her but she couldn't ring him. Their contact was between these hours on those days, regular as clockwork. She could join him at some conferences but not others because his wife was there. Months turned into years. Excitement turned into a comfortable love between them. But then the love became soured by her longing for him to be hers. She learned the hard way that human beings can't be emotionally and physically intimate for months on end without wanting and needing each other in a committed, exclusive relationship. That's when she began to nag him and he began to lead her on.

'I'm so unhappy in my marriage,' he would say earnestly. The triangle had become clear. His wife was the persecutor. He was the victim. And she, Marian, would rescue him. How cosy it all seemed. But there was a 'but'.

'But I can't leave my wife right now. Not just yet. You'll have to be patient.' Always a reason. The kids. The financial situation. His need to get his business more profitable. After next winter. Then the winter after that. The winters came. The winters went. She felt cold and alone in her big bed. Obsessing over him. Imagining him making love to his wife as the cold winds rattled her roof.

Six years went by. More and more dramas erupted between them. She was becoming tired and embittered. It was slowly sinking in. The message she didn't want to know. He was never going to leave his wife. Never. So she did what all good suicide bombers do when the time has come. She pulled the pin on the affair. She sabotaged it. Mistresses always do. She began telephoning Tony at home. She knew his wife would be there. The enemy. The source of her misery. Marian escalated her demands on Tony. I have to see you now. It's urgent. Then Tony began to reject her. He became angry. He called her 'a *mad bitch'. He'd changed. The affair was a patient on life support systems and someone had to have the courage to pull the plug. She phoned the wife. Did she know that her husband had been having an affair for the past six years? Then she hung up and spent hours sobbing into her pillow.*

It had been the only way to force him into making a decision. But mistresses know that the odds are stacked against them. Married men hardly ever leave their wives and children. And when they do the chances of their next relationship working are next to zilch.

Marian had to grieve not only the loss of the handsome, firm Tony but also the six years of her life that she had spent waiting for him. Waiting for him to call. Waiting for him to come to the coffee shop. Waiting for him to leave his wife. Wasted years. Turning away the advances of the young, needy men who would have grown up one day and been good boyfriends for her. Perhaps even a husband. A whole lot of wasted time.

No, this isn't me moralising, just letting you know how ex-mistresses present to me as a psychiatrist. Sad and angry. Obsessing with regret about the day that they let a married man into their lives. You see, affairs follow a predictable eight-step process:

- ♦ the meeting. This is usually casual or accidental. They may work together. They don't often go out looking for each other.
- ♦ the getting to know each other. Mutual physical and emotional attraction. Slowly developing.
- ♦ the falling into bed. 'It just happened one night.' That's what they say.
- ♦ the comfortable co-existence. She doesn't seem to mind that he goes back to his wife after each of their clandestine

meetings. The illicit nature of it adds to the passion and eroticism. Stolen kisses and all that.

♦ the developing need. She holds him in her arms. He moves in her body. Of course she comes to need him. Watching him leave becomes more difficult. She begins to pressure him. He becomes good at making up excuses. Sometimes he can even fool himself that he will be with her soon. But his wife has the trump cards: marriage, stability and, most of all, his children.

♦ the souring. And this can take years.

♦ the sabotage. Someone stops the game, usually with three people suffering disastrous emotional consequences.

♦ the recovery. But do these three people ever *really* recover from the affair?

HOW TO DEAL WITH THE MISTRESS

At the risk of sounding like a preacher here, perhaps affairs are not too clever an idea. Sure, they happen. But so does sewage. Happen, I mean.

So tell him to save you all a whole lot of anguish and go back to his wife. That's where he's going to end up anyway.

 The murderer

Now that I've shattered all your illusions about the extra-marital affair, I'm afraid you'll just have to brace yourself for some more disappointment. This is about the murderer. Particularly the common-or-garden murderer and not the slick-backed-hair, handgun-with-silencer Al Pacino sort of murderer.

Here are four types of murderer. I'll work through them in turn. They are:

- the Hollywood murderer
- the kitchen murderer
- the mass murderer
- the nastiest of them all, the serial murderer.

CASE HISTORY

Louie the thug needed to get a message to the Gaberdino gang that he wasn't amused about them siphoning off profits from his downtown protection rackets. So he decided to 'whack' one of the head thugs, a mole-faced upstart by the name of Frank Scarfacio. Frank should've known that he was in danger. He shouldn't have gone to the basement carpark all alone. He shouldn't have greeted the dark figure who waited in the shadows. He should've worn a bullet-proof vest. But even that wouldn't have stopped the lead that split his head open.

Still, all that's history now. Like Louie himself, who was 'iced' in retribution only a few days later. Two men wandered into the barber shop when he was in the chair. All Louie saw was a flurry of overcoats as sawn-off shotguns were pulled out. Flying shards of broken mirror. Then the Pearly Gates and Saint Peter wearing a frown.

The Hollywood murder. Common in the movies. Uncommon in real life. Like really uncommon.

CASE HISTORY

Stanley and Marie were alcoholics. They lived a grotty life in a grotty boarding house. They drank cheap moselle and plenty of it. You'd know that they were around if you were down-wind of them. Personal hygiene was not one of their strong points.

One dark night, after a long binge at their nearby pub, they returned home to Grottsville. They were squabbling, as they often did, but this squabble was becoming loud and obnoxious. Someone shouted at them from a back-street window to shut up but Stanley just shouted back. Something to the effect of the complainant's parents having never been married. And Marie piped up that the complainant should 'just f*** off'.

They got home very drunk and very hungry. Stanley found some stale bread in the kitchen and began stuffing it into his mouth. Marie found him there and was annoyed that he had chosen not to share the only carbohydrates left in the house. She suggested, in nothing short of a scream, that his own parents had never been married and that he rated slightly lower than the scum that forms in an unflushed toilet bowl. Stanley, being one of intemperate habits and not renowned for his control of his temper immediately replied that she was a lousy f***. She could get her own bread, he pointed out, and he wished that she would then insert it into a uniquely female orifice. She lost what was left of her cool and pushed him. He threw himself at her and knocked her over, holding his hands at her throat for some indeterminate time.

When he awoke the next day he found that he had somehow managed to crawl to bed. It was damp since he had wet himself during the night and also been incontinent of faeces. He didn't feel too well, as one doesn't the morning after consuming a flagon of muscat, and just managed to get to the toilet bowl before he vomited.

Then he staggered around looking for Marie. He found her where he'd pushed her onto the kitchen floor. She was stone dead. He didn't have to touch her. He knew by the look in her half-closed, lifeless eyes and that mottled colour on her skin. 'Oh sh★★' he said to himself. Even his fuddled mind could comprehend that he was in big, big trouble.

The kitchen murder. Very common. Note the classical features. The murderer and victim are known to each other. The murder is committed at home. Alcohol is involved. So is anger and a history of violence. A dangerous recipe.

CASE HISTORY

Bernard was an odd character. Not something you could put your finger on. Just not very relaxed in a social environment. His tendency to twitch his shoulders didn't help. Sometimes impulsive. Definitely friendless. The only man at the bridge club who didn't bring a partner. A man with idiosyncratic, solitary pursuits. Like fly-fishing on the river. Or taking photographs of light aircraft down at the local aerodrome. Some of them he'd had framed, as if he'd owned and flown them himself. But he'd never been higher than the top of a ferris wheel. And he'd been alone then too. All very odd.

When Bernard became a mass murderer no one was surprised. They looked back on his life and went through his things. The photographs of aeroplanes. The way his underpants had been ironed and his socks placed in neat rows according to their colour. All very odd. People nodded their heads wisely and a psychologist, referred to by the newspaper as 'an expert on mass murderers' said that these killers were often odd, just like Bernard. What he failed to point out was that there were another twenty people in the town who were even stranger than Bernard and never hurt anyone.

What separated Bernard out was his sense of outrage. He'd become more than a little paranoid because he'd been rejected once too often. The bridge club had asked him not to come without a partner. But that excluded Bernard because none of his handful of 'friends' (more like acquaintances, they all said later) had any interest in bridge. Then he'd been asked to leave by the Rhododendron Society because he kept interrupting their meetings by putting forward motions the contents of which were becoming stranger and stranger. So he went home and dug up his rhododendron bushes. That was the last that anyone saw of him until The Day of the Murders. But Bernard hadn't 'disappeared'. He was at home. Spending all day brooding. Feeling his sense of outrage boiling. Boiling up. Boiling over. The Rhododendron Society. That had been the last straw. The camel's back was broken. And so was he. He paced up and down. He drank the cooking sherry and paced some more. He was being drawn to his fate. Inexorably. A train with no brakes. He knew what he had to do. His life amounted to nothing. It was time to go. But he'd take a few of these thankless bastards with him.

But which rifle? He had four, each well oiled and glistening in anticipation. It was his life's project and the purpose of their very existence. He had been sent. This was it, he said to himself over and over again. He had been given *these guns as part of the Plan. It would be a message to the world. He would do this and then they'd know. They'd know about the Bernards of this world. They'd know what respect meant. If you can't get it, take it.*

'If you can't get it, take it,' Bernard said to the grocer. 'What are you talking about, Bernard?' They were the last words of the unfortunate grocer, who'd sealed his own fate by being the honorary treasurer of That Society. Bernard shot him at point blank range. Right through the face, from nose to cranium. Then the grocer's assistant. Then a woman with a push-chair in the main street. Then her baby, to stop that infernal racket. Then the young women who came to shop windows to see what the commotion was. Then a policeman. Then another policeman. Then he put the barrel of his rifle into his mouth. He winced as it cut his hard palate. Then he pulled the trigger and it was All Over.

The mass murderer. Fairly uncommon but guaranteed to make the headlines. An odd, isolative personality with paranoid tendencies and a grudge against someone. But the grudge becomes generalised to all of society. A need to punish them. Brooding, then an explosion, then mass murder and then suicide. Often carried out on the murderer's own family. Throw in the Family Law Court and a custody battle and you've got an explosive recipe.

CASE HISTORY

Brian had been a taxi driver all his life. He'd been part of the push to increase security for taxi drivers after one of his colleagues was murdered by a deranged heroin addict who'd do anything for money. The irony of his demands for greater protection from passengers didn't escape Brian. By that time he'd already murdered six of his passengers. Carefully chosen passengers. Hailed by the roadside rather than ordered by phone. Nothing traceable. The passengers always had to be alone. No one was allowed to see them enter his cab, he made sure of that. And then a taxi driving around with a passenger, who'd notice? The best 'catches' were young single women who hailed a cab in seedy back streets in the small hours of the morning. They thought they were safer being in a cab than on the streets. How misguided they were.

He would pretend to get lost in the inner-city roads and then take a 'short-cut' through the park in the middle of town. Then he'd pull a knife on them. No point screaming in the middle of nowhere. Tape over the mouth. Hands tied behind the back. Move the car to a more secluded spot. Or drive it out of town to that place where even young lovers wouldn't think of going. Third dirt track on the left and into the forest for some fun. He would wait until dawn. He needed to see the fear on their faces. Then he would cut their clothes off and stand watching them as they screamed muffled pleas to him to stop. He needed to see their fear and feel it. It made him feel powerful and alive.

It touched something in him. Something deep within his being that felt cold and dead. But when he had this power of life and death over someone he felt whole again. This life that he would take. This would make him feel strong again, like the elixir of life. Their being would drain away, like blood on the cold earth, beneath the feverish stabbing of his knife. And as they breathed their last he would take their life into his own veins and feel the 'rush' of this power, this joy in being alive and powerful.

Then the ritual. After they were dead, and he tried to prolong their last moments as long as he could, he would become aware of his erection. The ritual. He would masturbate over the corpse, his penis feeling bigger and stronger than ever. Then he would cut a hole into the victim's abdomen and leave his body fluid there. Leaving behind semen but no fingerprints. Another conquest. Another seduction. Another murder. Another orgasm.

Then back to the semblance of normality. Reading with interest that another young woman's decomposing body had been found buried in a shallow grave in the forest. He would join in the chat over the tea-room table. Mutterances of agreement when his workmates said the police should get the bastard who's doing this. And what a sick mind he must have.

The serial murder. Nasty, warped minds. Mad in their own way. The interface between violence and libido. Your dying gasps for their sexual pleasure and feelings of empowerment. Not a very fair trade.

HOW TO DEAL WITH THE MURDERER

You don't. You get an organisation called the Police to do that. All you have to do is to stay out of the murderer's way. So:

- ◆ Don't cross any thugs with tommy guns.
- ◆ Don't hang around with short-tempered alcoholics.
- ◆ Don't go anywhere with odd men with knives, especially if you're a hitchhiker or a prostitute.
- ◆ And above all, never, ever join a Rhododendron Society.

The
traumatised

This is a section about Post-Traumatic Stress Disorder, or PTSD for short. This is the stuff of Vietnam veterans, prisoners of war, survivors of car accidents, bush fires, train crashes, etc. Get the message? People with this disorder have usually been in a very scary situation where the Grim Reaper has been beckoning with a bony finger.

One of the saddest things about the traumatised is that they know too much. They lose their innocence by being confronted with a violent end or being exposed to too much blood and guts. They can't play any more. When you meet them at those cocktail parties you like to attend, they can't make small talk. They are like one-eyed men in the land of the blind. They have seen what shouldn't be seen. They know about things that you and I choose not to see or watch on television news in the comfort of our own living room. They are old brains in young heads. And once they've experienced their trauma it's difficult for them to go back to the world of denial, where you and I live.

CASE HISTORY

Fiona didn't know it but when she jumped into a taxi on that cold dark morning she was about to experience the most terrifying six hours of her life. It was Brian's taxi, of course, and he was already plotting to make her his seventh victim. Already he could see the headlines. He was becoming known as the 'Blackjack', a distorted reference to Jack the Ripper, with whom he was increasingly compared.

She was young. She wasn't too plain, either. Just the way he liked them. Her youth and innocence would increase the horror in her eyes later when he showed her his knife. He would make her kiss it before he stabbed her the first time. Yes, that's what he'd do. He'd humiliate her. That would show her how powerful he was.

And so it started. Becoming 'lost'. A 'shortcut'. The knife. The tape over her mouth. Her look of terror. His look of delight. She knew who he was. She'd read the newspaper reports. She knew what was going to happen to her. She was trying hard not to vomit. She felt as if she was suffocating. She struggled to maintain her consciousness because part of her was trying to faint into oblivion where he could just get on with it and let her die.

But Fiona wasn't going to become a statistic. She had the presence of mind to use her tied hands to open the car door as he drove to the next secluded spot. She fell out of the taxi backwards, sustaining agonising fractures and abrasions as she hit the asphalt. By sheer fluke another car was travelling along not too far behind and she was 'rescued' by a couple of teenagers looking for a dark spot to park and make clumsy back-seat love.

She was forced to see Brian again. Once in an identification line-up. Once more in court. Perhaps it was a worthwhile experience. He didn't seem so big or powerful now. Just a greasy man with acne scars.

She was hailed as a heroine but she felt like the Living Dead. His face, the image of that knife. They haunted her. In *images in her mind. In memories. Whenever she saw a taxi cab she would tremble and sweat. She would sometimes wake screaming. He was safely in prison but in her nightmares he visited her again. That self-satisfied smile. His breathing that almost purred with the pleasure of anticipation. The anticipation of her blood warming the cold earth.*

There are four features to PTSD:

♦ the trauma. Usually, but not always, life-threatening. Or at least being confronted with the dead bodies of others, as happens to military personnel and rescue workers. This is now a source of some considerable debate since PTSD has become something of a bandwagon, particularly if you're a disgruntled employee trying to sue your employer. I have seen PTSD develop in over-worked, over-conscientious and unsupported staff, such as emergency workers, even if there was no real physical danger involved.

♦ the 'haunting'. The trauma comes back to haunt you. Nightmares, memories, things in your day-to-day life that 'trigger' them. Like the smell of vinyl and the tick of the taxi meter. Or the war veteran who hits the deck whenever a helicopter flies overhead.

♦ the avoidance. You'll do anything to avoid being reminded of the trauma. You'll certainly never travel in a taxi again and even getting into a car makes you testy. Or living near the army base perhaps. Or watching old war movies.

♦ the emotional reactions. Mostly anxiety. You startle easily. You're always scanning your environment like a sentry on guard duty. Waiting and watching for the next attack. And you've lost your ability to play. You feel detached from the mainstream of life. You've lost your sense of humour. Nothing is trivial or light-hearted any more. Life is a deadly serious process.

If elements of this description fit you, then get down to your doctor and talk about it. PTSD is one of the most under-diagnosed and under-treated of all psychiatric disorders. And it can become complicated by a variety of factors:

♦ other anxiety disorders, since they occur in multiples, like birds of a feather
♦ strain in relationships, mostly because people have little or no understanding of what you've been through and continue to suffer
♦ depression, because if you're anxious enough or angry enough for long enough, you'll get depressed. Nothing surer.

And the treatment? Brace yourself. You're not going to like this. The treatment is centred on the need to return to the trauma. No, that doesn't mean that you have to hop into a cab with another knife-wielding murderer. It means that, given the right professional environment and some trust in your therapist you have to think back again and again over your trauma. Throw in some anxiety-reduction techniques and the trauma usually becomes much more manageable, even if it doesn't go away.

A final thought on the subject. There has been an increasing amount of interest recently in a treatment for this condition, which is called EMDR. That stands for Eye Movement Desensitisation and Reprocessing. It involves recalling distressing memories of the trauma and having your therapist move his finger back and forwards across your field of vision while you follow the finger with your gaze. Sound a bit peculiar? I tend to agree. Sounds a bit too much like snake oil to me, but then again the proponents of this technique swear by it. Perhaps the jury is still 'out' on this issue.

Enough about Trauma. Now let's consider a quiet, permanent trauma that some people carry all their lives. Let's look at Fat . . .

 The Fat

Never in the field of human endeavour has there been such prejudice against such a large group by most of the human race. Unless, of course, you live in some parts of the Third World, where being fat is associated with wealth, status and being really, really cool. For the rest of us it's definitely a no-no to be fat. In fact the pages of glossy magazines give up the message: women are supposed to be emaciated and men are supposed to be muscle-bound.

Have we lost our minds or what?

Get the message. Some people are just fat, that's all. They don't conform to the 'before' and 'after' photos in the slimming clinics' advertisements. They just stay looking 'before'. It's the way they were destined to be from the moment the fat little sperm hit the fat little egg. It's in their genes and their constitutions. Fat. That's the way they've always been and, famine notwithstanding, that's the way they'll be when they get squeezed into their over-sized coffins. Fat.

So give them a break.

CASE HISTORY

In medicine the Standard Man is affectionately known as 'Stan'. Stan weighs seventy kilograms, or about eleven stone. Charlie weighed three times that. Charlie didn't choose to be fat. He just was. He would've preferred to be thin. He would've preferred to fit through the door of a bus but he couldn't. Sometimes he would've preferred to have never been born.

He tired of the euphemisms. 'Cuddly'. 'Fuller-figured'. 'Abdominally challenged'. He came to prefer the plain term: 'fat'. That's how he was. And if he used that word he could turn his pain into humour. He earned people's affection by throwing off at himself. Self-deprecation. He could rattle off all the fat jokes. But there was a big flavour of pathos in it.

But Charlie was also faced with the realities of his size. Like finding big clothes. Sweating all the time (so unattractive!) Strain on his heart and lungs. Facing a life that would be a fair few years shorter than his contemporaries. Chafing beneath his folds of skin and with the rubbing of his thighs. Getting doctors to take him seriously. 'Of course you'll have to lose some of that weight,' they would say to him sternly. It seemed as if they were blaming him. The unspoken words were 'How did you let yourself end up like this?' He told himself that he didn't choose this. He told himself that he shouldn't feel guilty. But the way those doctors looked at him. There was a tone of disgust in their voices. Just like the look of disgust that he sensed from people in supermarkets. And the kids who were too young to know about politeness and would stare at him. 'Look at that big fat guy' he would hear them say. And then they would laugh at him, as kids do, so honest but so cruel.

Charlie had some other important life issues. Not just finding a really long belt with a strong buckle. Not just finding the perfect diet. But finding some self-respect. And someone who would see the lonely man beneath the layers. Someone some day who might even learn to love him.

In the end he found her cooking steaks at the local pub. She was no oil painting and needed a whole lot of dental work, but she had a hearty laugh and a way with food. *Perfect*, thought Charlie. So he made some clumsy approaches to her and blushed when he asked her to have a drink with him when she'd finished her shift. She was equally bashful at first, but a few quick beers gave them both a bit of Dutch courage and they spent many hours that night talking, laughing and enjoying each other's company. No fairy tale endings. No galloping off into the sunset. Just a couple of people finding each other out of all those other millions. They went out pretty often after that. They grew to love each other. He was stable and earned an income. The sex had been clumsy for the first few months. Charlie was trying too hard. But she found how to make him relax and in the end they both got some pleasure from it. With her on top. Otherwise she felt crushed by him. Nevertheless being Mrs Charlie was much, much better than her previous life of poverty and despair.

She tried to get him to diet but he refused. He'd done all the diets. All of them. He started off doing the crash diets that promise to lose bucketsful of lard in just a few days. He put the bucketsful back on just as quickly as they'd disappeared. Then he'd try the slow, sensible diets but his fat would creep back to grab him whenever he became complacent. And you can't be on guard against marauding fat all your life.

So that's how they lived. Not an easy life. They fought and hurt each other from time to time. But they could heal the wounds as well. A good enough arrangement. She needing security and he needing company to stave off the loneliness. Both refugees from the hardship of their lives.

Lay off the podgy. Some people are just fat. They were fat kids and they'll die fat. That's just the way they are. Don't stare at them. And don't snigger.

If you *are* fat then this exercise is for you:

❶ Go and look at yourself in the mirror.
❷ Now kiss your own reflection.
❸ Now go and have a cream bun and forget about those silly diets. Life is here to enjoy.

The pervert

If you've opened this book, scanned the contents and gone straight to this page you're probably pretty normal. We human beings have such a curiosity about anything sexual. This section is about how our sexual behaviour can become a little, shall we say, unconventional. After all we're led to believe that sexual intercourse is something to be carried out between consenting adults, behind closed doors, under the bedclothes, in the dark and preferably very, very quietly. Then one day we find ourselves hanging off a chandelier wearing the upper half of an ape suit and realise what fun that can be. So brace yourselves. Here are some 'behaviours' that are even more colourful . . .

consider this

You live in a high-rise apartment. It hasn't been designed that well because your kitchen overlooks your neighbour's bedroom. One night you're up to your elbows in suds at the kitchen sink when you hear a groaning noise, as if someone's in pain. You're about to call an ambulance when you see them. Your neighbours are doing it. You know, It. You didn't know that human bodies could be so flexible. Or that leather could be used for such a purpose.

Do you:

a. Phone your neighbours and respectfully suggest that they close their bedroom curtains?

b. Turn off your kitchen light and go and find your binoculars?

c. Do (b) and then make sure that you have an astronomical telescope set up on your kitchen bench, for future opportunities?

d. Do (c) and then go and prowl the neighbourhood on hot summer nights?

Diagnosis: voyeurism. The rationale behind peep shows and those really interesting glossy photographs in men's magazines. Isn't leather a many-splendoured thing?

CASE HISTORY
_____

Craig caught the train into the city every morning dressed in his business suit. He particularly liked rush hour. He would position himself standing up in a crowded railway carriage and then rub himself against women passengers. And when I say 'rub himself' you know exactly which part of himself he would rub. Startled women would slowly come to realise what he was doing. Usually they would give him a dirty look and move away. Once or twice they made a real commotion and slapped his face but they never made a police report about it.

That's why he was back there the next day. Every rush hour. To get his rush.

Diagnosis: *frotteurism. The behaviour of rubbing one's genitalia against an unknown person in a public place, for the purpose of sexual stimulation. We're getting kinkier here. And more offensive.*

C A S E   H I S T O R Y

Maurice was the finance manager of a large multinational corporation. He died accidentally. Then news got out of how Maurice's body had been found. He'd been wearing women's clothes and had his head in a plastic bag. Evidently this had been his way of obtaining sexual pleasure: the slinky, erotic feel of silk, lace and nylon stockings. Capped off with the hypoxia of nearly suffocating. But this time he'd gone too far and passed out. Maurice didn't do his 'thing' in the company of anyone else, so there was no one there to save him when he went blue.

What no one noticed was that Maurice had no 'male' underwear in his drawers. Just women's knickers. He preferred the feeling of them. He'd always worn them, even to those stuffy boardroom meetings where he'd have to get up and present the figures for the most recent quarter. Perhaps it had been his little joke.

Diagnosis: *transvestic fetishism. An odd behaviour displayed almost exclusively by heterosexual males. Just because they like to dress up in women's clothing doesn't mean to say they're homosexual in orientation. Don't ask me to explain all this stuff. I'm just telling you the way it is.*

Charles was a really straight accountant. (Don't fall for the old misconceptions that accountants are always really straight. Some of the most 'bent' people I know are accountants . . .) Charles had a monthly appointment at his local brothel. It was a little pleasure that he allowed himself. His wife thought that he had a regular meeting with a big client at those times. Instead he had a regular meeting with a red-headed woman who called herself 'Flame', although her real name was Irma.

Flame would put a dog collar on him and then lead him around the room. Then he'd have to sit up and beg. But the part Charles liked was when Flame would hit him with her leather strap for being a 'bad boy'. That was really exciting. But the 'crescendo' (for want of a better word) wouldn't occur until Flame mocked him and told him that he had a very, very small penis for a dog of his age.

After a bit more humiliation and mockery and some unusual activity with the aforementioned penis, Charles would get back into his business suit, return to his homely wife and get back to the world of figures, tax returns and suburbia. Talk about a double life.

Diagnosis: *sexual masochism. Once again, I'm just telling it like it is.*

The list goes on and on. Check out these definitions:

- ♦ necrophilia is for when you don't want your lover to talk back to you
- ♦ exhibitionism is a game played by men in overcoats and women with hairnets and shopping trolleys

- coprophilia involves too many bodily functions to be described tastefully
- zoophilia is also known as 'barnyard fun'
- paedophilia, as we all know, is the nastiest of them all
- and so on . . .

HOW TO DEAL WITH THE PERVERT

Q: When does a quirky sexual practice become a perversion?
A: When it hurts someone.

There is a general rule in our society. The civil libertarians scream it from the rooftops. It says that if you're not hurting yourself or others then you can do what you bloody well like. That means that if you're a hairy-legged bloke with a bushy moustache and you want to wear high heels in the privacy of your own home then go for it. However, if you're the same bloke and you like to hang around kids' playgrounds, then you can expect the full weight of society's contempt to descend upon you. So watch out for lynch mobs.

 The brain-damaged

Every medical student hates the time in their training when they must study neurology. That's the branch of medicine involved with the brain and nerves. It's just so damned complicated. Like being intimate with the position of every road and every back alley on the map of the world. It also confronts us with how vulnerable our grey matter is. Just a few days in hospital wards filled with car accident victims, stroke victims and the chronic, progressive destruction of their nervous systems is enough to make you wear a seatbelt and a helmet and look after your cranium. After all, it's the only one you've got.

Nervous tissue, you'll discover, doesn't regenerate itself nearly as well as most other tissues. If you sever your spinal cord, don't expect some surgeon with good eyesight to sew it back together again. And if you block or burst a blood vessel in your brain (as occurs in strokes) then say *sayonara* to that piece of brain.

CASE HISTORY
___

Once again, this is a true story. It's the tale of Phineas Gage. Phineas who? Read on.

Gage. Phineas Gage. He was a famous character in psychiatric folklore. Not because he discovered anything or became a professor at a world-renowned clinic. No, Phineas became famous because he lost his frontal lobes while labouring for the railways. No kidding.

He was working on a railway in Vermont in 1848. He was detonating a charge, presumably to clear a path for more rails, when a piece of metal flew up and embedded itself in Phineas' skull. In fact it went through his left cheek, up through his frontal lobes and out the top of his skull. Miraculously, he survived. A piece of American railway metal did in a trice what neurosurgeons would take hours at. It effectively cut off his frontal lobes from the rest of his brain.

Now the problem here is that you need your frontal lobes. Desperately, in fact. They are busy little lobes of gunk that you use during your every waking hour. This is where your learned socialisation behaviour resides. And your impulse control. It's where you plan for the future and originate goal-directed behaviour. It's where large elements of your personality exist. In psychiatry we learned a long time ago that 'you are your frontal lobes'.

In the bad old days of psychiatric asylums of sixty years ago there was a craze for chopping off patients' frontal lobes. Not that all the psychiatrists had gone mad. They'd discovered that in these pre-modern-medication days that very tormented patients would feel a lot calmer if they had the inside aspect of their frontal lobes cut off. So over-enthusiastic doctors spent many hours poking nail-like instruments up through the thin part of the skull just below the eyebrow, jiggling it around and then pulling it out. The patient would go through the rest of their lives sans frontal lobes. That wasn't such a bad deal if it transformed you from an agitated, obsessive, tortured soul into someone who could sit quietly and ignore the voices. But then doctors became a little over-enthusiastic and that meant that if you were anywhere near a psychiatric hospital, your frontal lobes got the chop.

Gage, on the other hand, didn't get the inside of his frontal lobes delicately dissected. On the contrary, he got a whacking great piece of uninvited railways metal right through the outside of his frontal lobes. Rather than his anxiety levels being reduced he became disinhibited. His usual social anxieties, the things that make you behave yourself, make idle chit-chat at cocktail parties and stop you from rudely staring at fat people was gone. Kaput.

So Gage spent the rest of his life wandering around the country annoying people. He insulted people to their faces. He pinched women's bottoms. He played silly practical jokes. This disinhibition is referred to by the German expression Witzelsucht, *which roughly translates as 'hypofrontal fool'. He was transformed from a conscientious railway worker (if such a thing exists) into a nerd extraordinaire. His personality was gone.*

I'm prompted to record this interesting saga because I read about Phineas in the newspaper recently. They'd dug up his bones, you see, to look at his skull. They needed to confirm that his personality change had been the result of frontal lobe damage, as had been suspected over all these decades. It was, they found. Then they laid Phineas' bones back to rest, another historical medical case confirmed. But not much consolation to the poor, unfortunate, brain-damaged Gage.

CASE HISTORY

Nora was a little old lady who lived in a little old house in a little old town. Nora refused to leave her home even though her husband Ernie had died two decades previously and she was touching seventy-five. Go into a retirement village, her family had told her, you'll be looked after well there. Just leave me here, she'd say. It's been my home for the past forty years, she said, and the only way I'll be leaving this house will be in a coffin.

What Nora didn't tell her family was that she was losing her memory. She also tried to deny it to herself. We all have day-dreamy times when we go into a room and forget what the devil we've come into this room for. But Nora did it often. Like four times a day. And she'd found she had to make lists. Even if she went down to the corner shop to buy three items, she'd have to write them down. If she could remember where she'd left the blasted pen and paper.

Nora was dementing, you see. In the early stages of Alzheimer's disease. We doctors all fantasise about finding a new illness and putting our names to it. Dunn's syndrome. What a nice ring that has to it. But Alzheimer, whoever he was, put his name to a particularly nasty one. This is a progressive illness in which one's brain cells die and we know by now that we just don't grow a whole lot of new ones to replace those. No, our brains just shrink and our mental processes steadily pack up and go west.

It starts with short-term memory. Like what did I come into this room for? Or why am I down at the shops with my shopping basket? Then it becomes 'What day is it today?'

Around this time Nora took great comfort in the fact that her long-term memory was perfectly intact. She could remember her childhood as if it were yesterday. If her family ever caught her out, she'd retort immediately that she could remember their birthdays and how they'd done at school. Trouble was, that was forty years ago. And Nora couldn't remember what she'd done forty minutes ago.

Dementing patients do similar things. They make their life ordered and predictable. They keep the scissors and the shampoo in regimented place. They learn pretty quickly that if they don't, they'll never find those items again. And they write down lists to aid their failing memories.

Another thing they do is to go into denial. They refuse to admit that there's anything wrong with their memories and they can always come up with beautiful rationalisations for why they should forget things or become confused. But somewhere in their hearts they know that they're losing their marbles and it terrifies the living daylights out of them. Because human beings probably fear dementia and madness more than death. This, we all know, can be the living death.

Alzheimer's patients try to conceal their illness as long as they can. But they can't do it indefinitely. It's a relentless disorder and King Canute fantasies don't impede its deadly work. Nora ended up in a nursing home. She'd become unable to look after herself and her GP had taken control of the situation. The family had taken her away, complaining and threatening loudly. Getting disorganised and hypofrontal by now.

She deteriorated rapidly after being taken from her home. Victims of Alzheimer's disease always do. They can't cope with being removed from the only environment they can control. In the nursing home she didn't know where the scissors or the shampoo were. Seven months later she was just a shell of the woman she'd been. The lively spark was gone. The photos of her as a beautiful young woman cradling her newborn baby bore no resemblance to the haggard, dribbling old patient in the stained hospital gown. Eight months later she was dead. And for her family grief but relief.

Maybe that's the hardest things about dementia. For the first half of your illness you suffer. For the second half your family suffers. Because the 'you' they remember is no longer there.

As they took Nora's body from the nursing home there was a commotion downstairs in the locked ward. Now most of us use locks to keep people out but the Downstairs Ward was a bit like a prison. The locks were used to keep people in.

Harold had punched someone again. He tended to do this and the staff were thoroughly fed up with it. The matron rolled her eyes and went downstairs to sort it out. She knew it would be Harold. He was the most difficult patient of them all.

Harold had been a prize-fighter. He'd spent his life in the ring. I don't know why they call it that since it's square, but there you have it. Harold had been damned good. Many a referee had held Harold's gloved hand high in triumph before the cheering fans. Even to the point of medals, trophies, championships. Some sort of primitive, animalistic, gladitorial tradition by which groups of human beings derive pleasure from watching other human beings enact violence against each other. Harold was paid good money for what he'd learned to do as a streetwise kid in dark laneways.

But now Harold the Champ was Harold the Dement. Dementia pugilistica. An uncommon disorder reserved for that exclusive band of men who repeatedly bash their heads on the fists of others. And how did Harold's dementia reveal itself? His frontal lobes were worn out so he expressed himself the only way he knew how: with his fists.

The matron arrived with an injection and poor Harold was returned to his chemical strait-jacket.

Once again, this is one for the medical profession. And a whole team of paramedical supporters like nurses and rehabilitators and occupational therapists.

If your loved one is brain-damaged then all you can do is be patient. After strokes or brain trauma you won't know for a couple more years just how permanent the damage will be. In general younger people heal better and some people make absolutely miraculous recoveries. On the other hand there is an entire subculture of people with jaded brains who are locked away in nursing homes.

You're allowed to grieve. To lose your brain is to lose your mind is to lose your spirit is to lose your self.

 # The abused

No one *has* the perfect parents. No one *is* the perfect parent. Agreed. But this section is about adults who were abused as kids. I'm not talking about being yelled at or told off here. I'm talking about capital 'A' Abuse. The inhuman stuff. The type that we psychiatrists try to mop up after every day of our working lives.

I'll focus here on sexual abuse, but it can also be physical, emotional or a combination of the three. In fact it usually is.

Case history

Glenda was being treated for depression. Not just a bad hair day. This was heavy-duty clinical depression. Early morning wakening, panic attacks, suicidal thoughts. The real McCoy.

It wasn't until she was beginning to improve that she decided to talk to her psychiatrist about what had happened to her when she was a little girl. She'd 'sussed' out her psychiatrist by then and felt she could trust this woman with the greying hair and the horn-rimmed spectacles.

So in session number eight, out it came. Her grandfather had done it. Her beloved grandfather. Respected and revered by all until the day he died. Glenda had gone to stay with her grandparents often. Her mother couldn't understand why she'd become increasingly broody and tearful. Her grades at school had fallen off and she spent much of her time in the playground alone. Once or twice she'd been found hiding behind a chair in the living-room, especially when it'd come time for her to stay at Grandma's again. Glenda's mother had never understood this out-of-character behaviour and had decided that it was 'a phase' that she was going through. Anyway Glenda's mum had enough problems of her own. She loved Glenda dearly, but Glenda's father hadn't stuck around and she had to go to earn a living working in the city. So Grandma and Grandpa had to be called upon often. At least they were a constant source of support.

Grandpa would take Glenda to his shed. It would happen there. Of course he would tell Glenda that no one must know about the games she played with him. With that part of him. No one must know. Or he'd never be able to see her again and her mother would lose her job and Glenda would have to go to live with her father who was in prison. And the prison inmates would do the same thing to her all day every day. So this is just our little secret, okay? Just our little secret. Just the way we love each other.

Glenda was only six. She couldn't put this together in her head. Even if it was too old for her shoulders. How could this man, whom she loved dearly, do this to her? He said it was all right. Just the way they loved each other. But she knew from the first visit to the shed that this didn't feel right at all. Kids always do know. It feels bad. Creepy. Yukky. And it hurts.

One day Glenda was found in the playground with one of the boys in her class. Glenda had her dress pulled up and her knickers down and she was groping little Timmy between the legs. The teacher who found them was aghast. Was this just playing 'doctors and nurses'? A bit too gross for that. And the kids were too old. So he told Glenda's mum. This led to a 'little chat' that night. Was anyone interfering with Glenda? Did anyone touch her between the legs? No, Glenda said. No one. She thought of her father in jail and all those convicts touching her too and she felt sick. No one had been touching her, she said.

Many years later she tried to bring the subject up with her mother again. But when she realised how fragile her mother was and how many problems she had, Glenda changed her mind. It had been clumsy and her mother had responded in an irritated way, not realising what her daughter was trying to say. So Glenda learned to shut up even though she had this dirty secret busting to get out. Until that day in session number eight, when she blurted it out to her psychiatrist. And a *frightened little girl within her waited for the psychiatrist to say that she must go to jail and be molested by rows of men in denim. 'Oh, dear,' said the grey-haired woman. 'I'd better hear more about this. Go on . . . '*

Glenda had found ways of coping with it. She had dissociated sometimes, so that she was in a trance as Grandpa abused her. Or out of her body, standing at the door to the shed watching 'them', her grandfather and her own body. For quite a few years she 'forgot' that it happened. Until she was eighteen. Then she had a torrid love affair with a young man at work and he asked her to do what Grandpa had asked her to do. Then she remembered.

She'd run into all the predictable problems suffered by the Abused. Some elements of Post-Traumatic Stress Disorder. A poor sense of personal boundaries. A phase of being promiscuous with narcissistic men. Sadists sometimes. A sad attempt to re-create her abusive relationship with Grandpa. In the vain hope of finding a nice grandpa, the one she'd loved. The one she wanted back, now in the form of truck drivers who'd pick her up while she was hitchhiking. Twice she'd been raped. But then it hadn't been wise to be where she'd been and to have got into those cars with those men.

She hated herself. Deeply, endlessly, continuously. And there were long phases of depression. Until session number eight.

Her healing took four years of therapy. Even then she knew that she would bear the scars. Even then she had to struggle to learn who was trustworthy and who was abusive. A slow process of reconstructing boundaries that had been defiled and broken down.

What more is there to say? Sexual abuse is terribly common and no victim escapes unscathed. Its consequences reverberate cruelly, like an echoed insult, through the life of the Abused. Self-worth, identity, boundaries, comfort with sexuality, relationships, moods. The things that you and I have enough struggle in developing become almost impossible for the Abused. This is the sort of stuff that can take years of painful therapy to even begin to address.

And a word to paedophiles: don't bother voicing your rationalisations about how your victims enjoy their experiences with you or how this is just another form of sexual expression. You do indescribable damage to the children you abuse. You are beneath contempt.

 the traveller

This is a section about comings and goings. That's different from going and staying away. If you go and stay away you leave the people behind to grieve for you. Flick back to the section on the Grief-stricken. But what if you keep coming back? In a peculiar way that's much more difficult for everyone to handle. But it's the situation that most military and airline families face frequently. The father in these families keeps disappearing for days or months at a time. He's absent. That's hard enough. Then he keeps coming back. That's even harder.

CASE HISTORY

Once again, this is a true story. But this time it's not about a fictional patient. It's about a monkey. Let's call him Ralph. He was the subject of study of an American behavioural psychologist called Harlow. Harlow made himself famous by observing the behaviour of monkeys. Let's face it, I could think of better things to be famous for . . .

Anyway Ralph was a baby monkey and Harlow had him in a cage with his mother. Harlow, who must have been a little on the sadistic side, decided to remove Ralph's mother from the cage and see what Ralph would do. Once again, I could think of better things to do on a rainy Wednesday afternoon.

Ralph displayed three distinct phases of reaction to the loss of his mother. First he bounced around the cage in panic, calling out for his lost mother. He shook the bars, he bared his baby teeth, he moaned and wailed. The stage of protest, wrote a satisfied Harlow in his journals.

Then Ralph slumped into a corner of his cage, hugging himself in a feeble monkeyish attempt to derive comfort. The sort of comfort that he'd usually get from his recently departed mater. The phase of despair, wrote a smiling Harlow.

Then Ralph got on with life. He emerged from the corner of the cage and wandered around, trying to kill time and find something to amuse himself. The phase of resolution. Harlow was having a very good day.

Then Harlow relented. He returned Ralph's mother to the cage. Now this was where Ralph was supposed to rush up to his mother, embrace her, express primate messages of happiness and relief and then get on with the task of being a baby monkey. You know. Bananas, fleas, peanuts. That stuff. But did Ralph do this? Nope. He rushed over to his mother and attacked her. The message, in monkey language, was 'How dare *you abandon me?!' There he was, this peeved little monkey, trying to beat up his mum. Of course this stage didn't last long. But Ralph had to get it out of his system before he could settle back to just being Ralph the baby monkey again.*

Now let's look at Angela. Angela's not a monkey. She's a housewife. And her husband George is an airline pilot.

CASE HISTORY

George was flying to Tokyo so he'd be away for the next two weeks. He hated leaving Angela and their two kids but this was part of his job. There had been dozens of times when they'd had to kiss and say goodbye. Before the kids arrived Angela had accepted it more graciously. But now she could really do with George's help around the house. And someone to take the kids off her hands before they became statistics in a children's hospital.

Now Angela hated his departures. How many more years of this would she have to bear? How many more farewells? There were times when she wished that his 747 would fall from the sky in a blazing wreck. Her next husband, she decided, would have a nine-to-five job and be home each evening. As in normal families.

But saying goodbye wasn't the hard part. The really awful experience occurred when he came home again. It was always the same. He'd be tired and jet-lagged. And he'd been faithful to her all these years. So he'd come home ready to hop into the sack and make passionate love. She, on the other hand, couldn't stand his touch. She was like Ralph. Angry as all hell. It would take a day or two for this to settle down. Her resentment at his comings and goings would smoulder all that time. Then she would usually weep. Quietly to herself. Her tears were from years of frustration. It was only then that they could come together. She would need him to hold her and soothe her. She would lower her defences and let him in again. And he would have his way. That was the pattern. Year after year.

The goings were hard but the comings were harder.

In this day and age families are increasingly disrupted by the need for one member of the family to be away from home. Regularly and for protracted periods. It takes its toll on families. Compassionate corporations had better realise that.

HOW TO DEAL WITH THE TRAVELLER

If you're young and harbouring a dream of piloting large aircraft across vast stretches of ocean, then keep in mind that you are going to doom yourself and your family to repeated upheavals. The comings and the goings. Ditto for anyone in the military or one of the sell-your-soul corporations in which you're expected to clock up frequent flyer points. Also for any travelling sales-person who has to go out of town regularly.

For the traveller I can only offer my sympathy and suggest that you:

♦ Spend as little time as possible away from the family.
♦ Let them get used to the fact that you've returned and don't expect to simply re-assume your position as the 'head of the family' or whatever. Remember, you've shown over and over again that you're dispensable.
♦ When you do come home, don't expect that the second bang you'll hear will be the door closing behind you. Think about it.

If you're the Angela in this scenario then you're allowed to expect some time to adjust once your George comes home. Be patient with him. It's part of his life and *ergo* part of yours too.

 The Lost

I do not mean geographical loss here. I'm not referring to people who can't find their car in the shopping mall carpark, I'm talking about people who can't find their way in life, who are existentially lost. Their meaning, purpose, identity, direction. You know, navel-gazing stuff. The Meaning of Life.

There are a number of times in your life when you're going to run into a great big crisis. You'll agonise over all these nebulous but terribly important issues. In fact how many times will you have to do this? Three times, that's how many. Three life crises. And here they are:

❶ The adolescent crisis. The question to be asked is '*Who will I be?*'
❷ The mid-life crisis. The question to be asked is '*Who am I?*'
❸ The death-bed crisis. The question to be asked is '*Who was I?*'

Now as you're digesting these momentous concepts I'll dazzle you with some case histories.

CASE HISTORY

At the age of eighteen, Christian realised just how much he hated his name. Sure it was hip and trendy. Like Christian

Slater, heart-throb extraordinaire. Trouble was that he'd just decided to become a Buddhist. A few of his arty-farty pinko-liberal peers had decided that this was the cool thing to do. Sort of Eastern and mystical. What a great way to pull the chicks. But a Buddhist called Christian? Yet another reason to hate his parents. For being middle-aged nerds who had imposed this awful name upon him.

Christian was into the environment, socialism, recreational drugs, the right brand of sunglasses and listening to bands in pubs. Christian was not into studying, parenthood, assuming any sort of responsibility or planning for the future. He had plenty of future. Stacks and stacks of years to live. He could dream about all the things that he could do with his life. Dammit, he might even become a Muslim at some stage. He'd look good in that garb that Muslims wear and he'd be prepared to sacrifice alcohol as long as he could smoke dope and have half a dozen nymphet wives who were all on the Pill.

So this was the superficial and totally egocentric world of Christian. A young adult, tormented by his adolescent ghosts, immature and silly at times, but his self-image was definitely adult. He wasn't a kid any more. And also trying to make the most of these young, supple days of narcissism and self-righteousness.

The thorn in the paw of Christian's happiness was, of course, his parents. He had come out of secondary school and now he faced the big crunch. What was he going to do with his life? Who was he going to be? On to tertiary education? Or go and find a job? Hours of tedium with lectures and *exams or the agony of job interviews and then years of being polite to some dictatorial boss? He fantasised of being able to run away from it all. To live in a little hut by the sea and go on the dole so that he could spend his days surfing and listening to pop music in the sun. And he spent many hours battling with his nerdish parents who were trying to pressure him to 'do something' with his life.*

CASE HISTORY

Christopher had gone to university and done his degree in business. Then he'd climbed the corporate ladder and here he stood, perched on a rung not far from the top, earning a good income, working seventy hours a week, sending his kids to expensive private schools and facing his fiftieth birthday. So why did he feel so unhappy? Why were these goals, that he had set for himself in his early twenties, providing him with no satisfaction? Why did he find himself fantasising about living in a little hut by the sea and facing sunny days with nothing much on his mind apart from casting a fishing line far out beyond the breaking waves?

When he was eighteen he'd thought that he would always have time. At school he'd studied T.S. Eliot and now he couldn't get the words out of his mind. 'And yet there will be time, there will be time.' The words rang in his ears. There wasn't time at all. He was running out of time. He'd passed half-way and he was thinking more and more these days about how he would die one day. What would that be like? What would it be like to take your last breath and your heart heave for one last time? He shuddered. He was getting old. He'd witnessed some of his colleagues leave their wives and run off with younger women. He'd had contempt for them then. Now he knew why they'd done it. They were trying to feel young again. They couldn't face the prospect of wrinkles and redundancy so they lost themselves in some erotic escapism offered by a sweet young thing with a father complex. Now Christopher was finding himself eyeing his own secretary and wondering what she would look like wearing nothing but lingerie and a smile.

Success had been his sacred cow and now it seemed futile; just some walking beef with ticks. What was the meaning of his life? It was a train that had skipped the tracks and was now lying on its side by the main trunk line of his life. He descended more and more into isolation and brooding. His wife became worried but couldn't get him to speak. He was, after all, a man. And men just don't speak about these things. Do they?

C A S E   H I S T O R Y

Colin had cancer. He knew that it would kill him. His kindly doctor had asked him whether he wanted all the facts at once. Colin replied that he did and then reeled at what he heard. The biopsy had confirmed that his liver was riddled with cancer. The doctor was reluctant to give an exact prognosis. Colin might have two months or he might have twelve. But he'd better get ready for his last birthday party. And he'd better do the 'getting your affairs in order' thing. That meant talking to the family, the accountant, the solicitor, the undertaker and the rabbi.

Colin spent a few days mulling over his sense of confusion, fear and anger. Then he decided that he'd better make the most of the time that he had. After all he was seventy-eight years *old, so he'd had a good innings. And it wasn't as if he'd never contemplated the prospect of his own death. He'd thought about it regularly since he'd gone through that awful depression in his late forties. He'd had that messy affair and then worked for years to try to get his wife to forgive him and ease his own guilt. Then his dearly loved brother had dropped dead from a heart attack and Colin had been a pall-bearer, carrying this man whom he had played and fought with to a cold, muddy hole in the ground. Then his wife had died, professing her love for him as she lay in that dreadful hospice. And he'd endured the years of painful adjustment to his loneliness and the feeling of cold in his bones on a winter morning.*

But now was the time to face his own End. He'd left his Jewish upbringing behind many years ago. Now he spent days thinking back over his life. Who he'd been. Who he'd loved. The things he'd achieved and the mistakes he'd made. He forgave himself for these. He knew that he hadn't been a bad person, just clumsy sometimes. He found himself thinking of the God of Abraham and Isaac. And a little hut by the sea where he could live in the sun and find peace.

So these are the three Life Crises. We all have to face all three. Unless we're lucky enough to be struck by lightning and then the third crisis occurs as your life flashes before your eyes before the oblivion washes over you. The Life Crises are like grief. A process to be worked through. They can't be ignored or hurried.

CASE HISTORY

So far the case histories in this book have been the products of my fertile and slightly warped imagination. Now here's one that happened. I know it happened because it happened to me. This is the story of Arthur, with whom I dug a ditch. Arthur was an old man then. He must be dead now. He had spent all his life as a labourer for the local council. His skin was tanned and scarred from too many bumps and scratches and too much sun. No sunscreen lotion when Arthur was a young man. He'd worked hard all his life. Earning his keep by the sweat of his brow. Now he was old and bald with a bit of grey hair and a pot belly from his devoted wife's home cooking.

I was a medical student. About Christian's age. Full of idealism and with no thought for the future apart from the dream of one day being some sort of doctor. I worked for the council during my 'holidays' since, like most university students, I lived on the bones of my backside and had to work to earn some money to survive the next semester.

One day Arthur and I were assigned to dig a ditch. We got talking. Arthur must've been in that third Life Crisis since he began to speak about all manner of philosophical issues. Within this funny little man's balding head was a brain that thought deeply and cut through the swathes of nonsense to go right to the heart of the matter. From the mouths of babes and contented old men. And the matter to be discussed over shovel-loads of clay was the Meaning of Life. No kidding.

Arthur told me that what people sought in life above all others was Peace of Mind. He was right of course. That's the Holy Grail. Peace of Mind. Through all the years of study, hanging around with arrogant academics who hide away in universities and think they know it all and all those professors *with all those letters after their names, no one taught me more in a such a short period of time than Arthur did. Peace of Mind. Learned in the time it takes to dig a ditch from here to there. You don't get it from what you have but from who you are and who loves you.*

Good old Arthur.

HOW TO DEAL WITH THE LOST

You can't do a whole lot to help the Lost to become the Found. The Lost have to find their own way out of it. We always do. Even if it means that we each fall off the rails from time to time. This is the Human Spirit. Get up off the floor and get on with it. Life, that is.

ЄPILOGUЄ

So there you have it. A grab-bag full of People, both Painful and Pain-full. By now you will have also recognised that many of these People overlap. Like the Psychopath who might also be a Liar or even a Murderer. And the Limpet who's also an Actress at times. In a peculiar way I feel that there's a bit of all these People in all of us. We're all painful at times and pain-full at others.

Now you've heard of interactive television. This is an interactive book. Or at least your chance to have a say in the Painful People who go into the sequel. Yes, I know I've just finished this one, but my ERB is getting at me already and I'm on a roll, so I might as well keep writing.

Let me know about the Painful and Pain-full People in your life. You can see the template that I've established here and I'm already hungry for more case histories. So get your ballpoints out or dust off the word processor. No prizes, just a chance to see your own 'PP' in print.

Send your ideas to:
More Painful People
PO Box 20/12 Blenheim Road
North Ryde, NSW, Australia, 2113

So don't just sit there, get writing . . .